MICHELLE OBAMA
FIRST·LADY·OF·FASHION·AND·STYLE

MICHELLE OBAMA
FIRST·LADY·OF·FASHION·AND·STYLE

SUSAN SWIMMER

BLACK DOG
& LEVENTHAL
PUBLISHERS
NEW YORK

Published by
Black Dog & Leventhal Publishers, Inc.
151 West 19th Street
New York, NY 10011
www.blackdogandleventhal.com

Distributed by
Workman Publishing Company
225 Varick Street
New York, NY 10014

Manufactured in the United States of America

Cover and interior design by Sheila Hart Design, Inc.

Cover photograph: Newscom
Back photographs: clockwise from top right: AP Images/Ted S. Warren: AP Images/Pablo Martinez Monsivais;
    Chip Somodevilla/Getty Images; Arnold Turner/Getty Images; Newscom; Shawn Thew/Corbis;
    AP Images/Jae C. Hong; UPI/Mike Theiler/Landov
    Additional photo credits can be found on page 128

Paperback Edition ISBN-13: 978-1-57912-826-5
    h g f e d c b a

Library of Congress Cataloging-in-Publication Data is on file at Black Dog & Leventhal Publishers, Inc.

ACKNOWLEDGMENTS

It takes a village, it was said by one previous First Lady (Hillary), and the writing of this book is no exception.

Thank you to Jen Braunschweiger, for asking the really important questions right up front, and to Rachel Wilk, for crack research that was done in a jiffy. My thanks go out to Elke Ridge, who gave me what I needed when I needed it most: a place to write and a babysitter I could depend on. Heartfelt thanks to Jonny Lichtenstein, whom I love and adore, for helping me pour over photographs and discuss every last detail (brooch!). Thanks to Lesley Seymour, whose guidance over these last fifteen years has been unwavering and unparalleled. There's no one I'd rather work for. My thanks to Regina Haymes for her ongoing tutorial on the artistry of great clothes, and a big thank-you to Tara Stewart, for cheering me on from the get-go. I want to thank my editor, Camille March, who first found me and then guided me through this process. It was a dream assignment. Thanks to my husband, James, for his enthusiasm, support, and fantastic edits, and to my daughters, Amelia and Simone, who (reluctantly) put playtime on hold so that I could write this book.

And finally, to our country's First Lady, Michelle Obama: I am one of the millions in your fan base who has waited a long time to have such a smart, successful, modern, stylish woman to admire. That I was given the opportunity to create this chronicle is the icing on the cake. My thanks to you.

TABLE OF CONTENTS

INTRODUCTION

The public fascination with First Lady Michelle Obama has developed gradually. She is a Harvard-educated lawyer, a successful executive, mother to two young girls, a devoted daughter and sister, the first African American First Lady, and wife to the president of the United States. She is beautiful and, at nearly six feet tall, a towering presence, but pre-2007 she was an unknown quantity to most of the American public. Her initial appearances, standing beside her energetic and charismatic husband, were measured. After all, a number of other women were being scrutinized early in the 2008 presidential campaign, and Michelle Obama's profile was downright discreet, whether by design (as some pundits believe) or simply because there wasn't any room for her in the media. It's hard to imagine that now, of course, but remember that there were many months of Hillary Clinton, Judith Nathan Giuliani (wife of Rudolph Giuliani, a Republican presidential candidate until January 2008, when he bowed out), and Cindy McCain—all three formidable women with their own style, and all three angling for airtime. Michelle Obama would have her time, but she'd have to wait.

The 2008 presidential election had one of the more protracted campaigns in history. The Democratic Party, ultimately torn between two strong candidates, divided the spotlight over the many months of debates and campaign stops. The political discourse was heated, at times antagonistic, and Barack Obama maintained the serious intensity the process required. Michelle, who was initially unenthusiastic about her husband's running for president, ventured into the campaign reluctantly. She shook a lot of hands but addressed crowds only occasionally. Critics harped on her for being detached, and also accused her of, when she did decide to speak publicly, sharing too much information: too many candid, off-the-cuff remarks about the Obama home life, such as volunteering her husband's lack of tidiness around the house. Her personal style was that of a corporate executive, which in fact she was. In 2002, she began working for the University of Chicago Hospitals, first as executive director of Community Affairs and then, beginning in May 2005, as vice president of Community

and External Affairs. She continued to hold the University of Chicago Hospitals position during the primary campaign, but eventually cut back to take part in her husband's election. Her affinity for power suits, boxy and structured and in a spectrum of dark colors, did little to inspire people's fashion imagination.

Michelle, a hands-on mom to two young girls as well as an executive, wanted to maintain the rhythm of that life as long as possible. Over time, as the campaign became more intense and more consuming, and as the likelihood of Barack's winning the White House loomed possible, Michelle became an important part of the operation. She took on a more visible role and became an integral part of Barack's message. Credited with writing her own stump speeches, she often spoke extemporaneously. Michelle developed her own speaking style (fewer wisecracks, more sentimental revelations) and also her own fashion sense—the armor of her corporate power wear slowly evolved into softer separates. But Michelle worked hard at maintaining some semblance of normalcy for her family during the pre-primary season. She and Barack had a deal: Michelle would spend no more than two days a week attending events, and she would only spend a night out of town if the girls could come along.

Eventually, her relaxed appearance and candid manner started to really resonate with voters and became the perfect balance to her husband. Barack, who had a focused manner, the cadences of a Baptist preacher, and a tendency toward the dry analytics of the constitutional law professor he had once been, was all business. Michelle's presence reminded people that he was a leader *and* a husband, a man with vision *and* a man who is reflective, a man who's tough *and* a man who's sentimental. It was Michelle who made him more accessible. As Michelle increasingly shed her corporate executive exterior, she revealed herself as a woman of warmth, sensitivity, and humor. Michelle became the emotional liaison between her husband and the voters he was trying to reach. It was subtle but intangible. *Tangibly* intangible: her faith in and commitment to him was contagious. If *she* believed in him, *we* could believe in him.

The campaign changed, of course, in August 2008, when only two men were left in the running. As divergent as Barack Obama and John McCain were, their wives were perhaps even a greater study in contrasts. Cindy McCain would never be overlooked; she was striking, after all, but it wasn't long before everyone—

Opposite, left: Early in the campaign, Michelle Obama was uninvolved. A busy executive, she continued working at the University of Chicago Hospitals until she stepped up to take a major role in her husband's campaign. Her look at the time, pictured here are a rally, consisted of the basics: black suits, turtlenecks, and her (then) trademark "flip" hairstyle. **Opposite, top right:** United States Democratic presidential hopeful Hillary Clinton arrives in Monterey, California, to hold a town hall meeting. After years spent supporting her husband throughout his twelve years as Arkansas governor and his two presidential terms, to say nothing of the pressure of being First Lady, Clinton fought hard to try to win the Democratic nomination. **Opposite, bottom right:** Cindy McCain, wife of Republican presidential nominee John McCain, was a very visible presence throughout her husband's campaign. Her look was polished—lots of crisp, silk suits—and although she and Michelle differed on many matters, they shared an affinity for bright colors.

everyone—started talking about Michelle Obama. In campaign stop after campaign stop, Michelle Obama stood beside her husband as he talked to Americans about hope and change, and she exuded a calm resolve. In an election that was often consumed with talk of sexism, racism, and the unavoidable realities of a country trapped in economic turmoil, Michelle came across as an integral element of her husband's momentum. She was attentive, empathetic, warm, and funny. In her, Barack Obama had a true life partner; in her, the country would have a woman of our times, just at the time when we needed her most.

The Obama family portrait began to captivate the American public. It's as if everyone let down his or her guard of jaded cynicism to take it in. In this age of high-speed everything, where portable gadgetry has made news and pop culture junkies out of all of us, the Obama family caused everybody to stop, look, and listen. There was a collective pause when they arrived on the scene and started talking, people everywhere took a break to *experience* the moment. The meaning was clear from the get-go: the Obamas would be a new family for a new America, representing everything that was forward thinking and contemporary. And at the same time, this power couple, eager to forge ahead, clearly held strong to their roots and the basic, common interests shared by all. Their message may have been about igniting the passion to change, but their sensitivities were clearly guided by the traditional values that Americans seemed to crave: hard work, integrity, and commit-

ment. They spoke of simpler times and timeless ideals. Of resolution, not conflict. Of getting involved, not giving up. This portrait of a young, vibrant, nuclear family, standing before a country on the brink of recession, saying they would lead the charge for a better future, was just the low-tech salve we the people needed to hear.

Not since the Kennedys had we felt it before, it has been opined. But comparing the Obamas to John and Jacqueline misses the mark in many ways. Camelot was storybook-like: unattainable and ethereal. It was coated with a film of naïveté—pretty, perfect, impenetrable, an aspirational tale that would never be realized by most, not by a long shot. Although this time of the Obamas has been dubbed "Bamalot" by some, it's a different rendition of that storied time. Just as Jackie Kennedy represented important ideals of the women of her generation, so does Michelle Obama. But the reality is that the times are very different. Everything about Michelle speaks to the modern postfeminist woman. She knows her mind and speaks it; she is guarded but genuine, both formidable and feminine. Her life choices have been directed by her passion, ability, and recognition of what really matters. Jackie's soft-spoken, wide-eyed gaze is in sharp contrast to Michelle Obama's steely focus. Jackie certainly did many good works, but the role she played most comfortably was that of dutiful wife, not the equal partner that Michelle seems to be. Michelle is her own woman. She is like me. She is like you.

There's a reason many of us relate to her. We "get" her, because we feel certain she "gets" us. She is a woman navigating

her way in extraordinary circumstances, and she handles it in the way we imagine we would on our best possible day. She has established herself, who she is and how she wants to be, but finding her place in the illustrious lineage of First Ladies will take time. If navigating the pressures of transitioning her family to a new house, deciding on the causes she most wants to champion, and making the numerous personal appearances required of her each week aren't enough, she also has to contend with all the clothes. Dressing the part is no easy feat. After all, Michelle Obama is not the first in her position whose every fashion choice is put under a microscope, and she surely won't be the last.

The first woman who had the opportunity to shoulder the responsibilities of becoming First Lady, Martha Washington, had her own treacherous journey trying to manage her public image. Martha was rich in her own right before she married George. Widowed in her mid-twenties, she was left a wealthy property owner by her first husband. She became Mrs. Washington when she was twenty-seven, and, with landholdings combined with his, they prospered. Martha liked to live well and was a known shopaholic, often traveling abroad to buy the latest couture. Once her husband was elected president, it wasn't long before the press skewered her for looking far too fancy. George's inner circle urged Martha to

First Lady Michelle Obama walks off Marine One as she and her family return to the White House in February 2009. Her ability to seem as comfortable at an official function as when she is relaxing with her family is something that really resonates with the public.

tone it down, to present an appearance more in keeping with how "real people" dressed, and she did. From then on she wore simpler things and also eliminated her habit of buying English couture (apart from appearing extravagant, it didn't play well that she was supporting the very economy that the colonies worked hard to break free from).

Mary Todd Lincoln, another clothes-horse, traveled regularly to New York City to stock her closets. She went on these shopping sprees regularly, and when her husband's $25,000-a-year salary didn't provide for her "habit," department stores extended her credit so as to keep her business. Word got out, and her "habit," particularly troubling at time when the Civil War was raging on and battlefield casualties mounted daily, became a political liability for her husband. The people were outraged, and accused the First Family of being poor role models, out of touch and insensitive. It has been reported that when Abraham Lincoln died, his widow had so much personal debt that she was forced to sell her clothes on consignment to be able to pay her bills.

In the early 1930s, when Louise "Lou" Hoover was First Lady, the coun-

Top: Martha Washington, First Lady to her husband, George Washington, had inherited extensive property holdings from her first husband, who died when she was in her mid-twenties. When George became president, Martha continued to dress in the manner to which she had become accustomed, but some thought it too fancy for a president's wife. Martha is shown here in an engraving that was made in 1872 from a painting.
Bottom: Mary Todd Lincoln, First Lady to Abraham Lincoln, was a known shopaholic of her time. She is shown here, in a photo taken in Springfield, Illinois, four years after she married Lincoln.

try's cotton industry was struggling. As First Lady, she was expected to help in the effort to rejuvenate the business. A photo session was staged at the White House, with Lou happily wearing styles of the times all made from American-produced cotton. The publicity stunt invigorated consumer confidence in that fiber (and in the president as well), sales increased, and Lou was heralded as a woman of the people and a style icon of the times. Eleanor Roosevelt, not a fashion plate by any standards, was the first First Lady to be photographed in a bathing suit, and the ensuing press frenzy on the "appropriateness" of such a risqué display percolated for weeks.

And then there was Jacqueline Kennedy, whose style came to define her. Jackie married into one of the most influential and powerful political families in America. Much was expected of her in terms of what she'd represent and how her image would affect her husband's political career. She defined refined elegance. She had studied art and culture, spoke French, and dressed impeccably. Her taste was developed over years spent shopping in the haute couture salons of Paris. Once she was First Lady, she is said to have worked with designers to create her look, involving herself in everything from pattern sketching to fabric selection.

The American public ate it up. A young, gorgeous family in the White House was a refreshing change of pace after FDR (who died in office), Truman (aged sixty-eight when he left office), and Ike (aged seventy when he left office, after suffering a heart attack while president, at age sixty-four). John and Jacqueline Kennedy were American royalty, and that image took hold in the collective American imagination like no other. The Kennedy publicity machine, in turn, worked overtime to get the message and the pictures out. It was all Jackie, all the time. Effortless daytime suits and sheaths set off with pearls, smart capri pants with cardigan sweaters topped with silk scarves for vacations, sleek evening attire perceived as understated elegance: sleeveless silk column dresses, opera-length gloves, diamonds. The Kennedys were the first First Couple to live out their lives in a United States where television was ubiquitous, after all, and the power of that medium was profound. Their image *was* the message: youth and taste for a bright, happy future. Everyone wanted to be them.

Not since Jackie Kennedy has a First Lady embodied such style. Not Lady Bird Johnson, whose time in the White House was first overshadowed by the tragic events that got her there, and then by an America gripped by the tragedy of the Vietnam War. Pat Nixon's fashion sense defined conservatism, labeled as such early in her husband's presidential career when her choice of outerwear, of all things, became the subject of one of her husband's most studied speeches. When, then Senator, Richard Nixon was named Dwight Eisenhower's running mate, questions arose regarding monies raised for Nixon's campaign expenditures. Eisenhower reportedly debated dropping the ambitious senator from the ticket, but feared that the change would alarm the voting public. What to do? In the now famous "Checkers speech" Nixon accounted for every dollar he and

Below: Nancy Reagan epitomized Hollywood glamour when she arrived at the White House with her husband, Ronald, in 1981. Known for an extravagant wardrobe, she also took it upon herself to overhaul the White House, redecorating many of the rooms, ordering new china, and commissioning artwork. Times were good then, and the American public seemed captivated by her. **Right:** At a National Garden gala in 1994, "A Tribute to American First Ladies," six former First Ladies were in attendance. They are, left to right: Nancy Reagan, Lady Bird Johnson, Hillary Rodham Clinton, Roslyn Carter, Betty Ford, and Barbara Bush. The women may have differed in style and ideals, but they certainly had a unique shared experience.

his wife had ever spent. "I should say this," Nixon said in the speech, "that Pat doesn't have a mink coat. But she does have a respectable Republican cloth coat, and I always tell her she would look good in anything." In one fell fashion swoop, Nixon's standing on the ticket, and political fortunes, were restored.

Betty Ford was no fashion maven, and was known then, and remembered now, more for her personal struggles than for any of the clothes she wore. Roslyn Carter eschewed all extravagances and was happily homespun, and the critics carped at her for her lack of style. The country did a collective about-face when Nancy Reagan arrived on the scene. She embodied Hollywood glamour, and flaunted it, too. Nancy caused a firestorm of sentiment regarding her focus on fashion. In Washington via Hollywood, with

Top: During her husband's presidency, Jacqueline Kennedy became a symbol of fashion for women all over the world. Her glamour was electric, her style imaginative, and the effect was brilliant. The "Jackie" look created a very feminine, confident, and elegant mystique. **Bottom left:** Coco Chanel was considered a designer ahead of her time. Her clothes were created for a modern sensibility, and women especially loved the ease and simplicity of her little black dress. It became all the rage and remains, to this day, a staple of women's wardrobes. **Bottom right:** Designer Donna Karan, who celebrated her twenty-fifth anniversary in business in 2009, is credited with single-handedly changing the way working women dress. To replace big, boxy suits, Karan devised a system of dressing that included lots of dark separates in shapely knits, asserting that women should wear styles that enhance their body instead of trying to hide themselves in menswear-inspired suiting.

her movie-star husband, she liked her glamour heavy handed. After four years of a very casual Roslyn Carter, Nancy determined it was her duty to restore formality and panache to the White House. She certainly dressed the part—her close relationships with top American and European designers were notorious. By the end of President Reagan's term, the economy was faltering. Nancy, ever the optimist, continued to put her most fashionable foot forward.

Barbara Bush? She was everyone's sensible, not fashionable, grandmother. She was sixty-four years old when she moved into the White House, and her style choices reflected her no-nonsense sensibility: primary colors and classic shapes. For her, fashion was a nonevent.

Hillary Clinton struggled with her personal identity as seen through the lens of fashion, and the American public watched her conflict play out in often excruciating detail. She was conflicted: she wanted to be taken seriously for the issues she championed, but she also wanted to be embraced as an everywoman. She wanted to be the career-driven superstar, but she wanted to be perceived as a doting mother. She wanted to be sleek and stylish, she wanted to be accessible. And as she vacillated between the many different roles she played, her fashion choices were equally mercurial. The more she fought America's desire to discuss her every hairstyle, the more the debate raged on. It's been reported that her husband's handlers held dozens of focus groups devoted to contemplating the First Lady's appearance, polling people on everything from her choice of colors to whether she should wear pants in public, and America's distaste never wavered. After trying on many hats, literally and figuratively, she eventually found her fashion sense of self (she now wears well-made pantsuits in a myriad of flattering hues).

Yes, First Lady fashion watching was always something of a national pastime, but in today's media-overloaded world, the documentation and discussion of such is ubiquitous. First Ladies have spawned trends from hairstyles and hats to handbags and suits. There have even been colors named after them, such as Eleanor (Roosevelt) Blue; Mamie (Eisenhower) Pink; and Reagan Red, after Nancy. First Ladies have always been mindful of the effect their fashion choices have, whether they enjoy it or not.

All people, famous or not, express themselves with what they wear, whether they intend to or not. A person running out for milk in the morning may not give a moment's thought to what to put on, but to everyone who sees that individual, a message is sent. That message may be interpreted differently, but it is sent nonetheless. There are, of course, varying degrees of interest in fashion. Some have more of an appetite for it than do others, some pursue it more creatively than do others, some devote more money to it than do others, but the reality is, we all have to get dressed every day. For some, fashion is a combination of means, needs, and creativity. For those of us without a personal press corps following our every move, clothes are a matter of personal preference, habit, occupation, culture, environment, practicality, or all of the above.

Learning how to navigate the racks isn't always easy. Colors are chic one season, out the next. Hemlines rise and fall. It's the year of the leg! The year of the waist! The year of the shoulder! Modern women have many choices—too many, some say—and a myriad of occasions for which they must dress. Women's fashion has evolved over time, and although it is an industry that has mainly been built and cultivated by men, there are many strong, assertive, smart women to thank for some of the truly great innovations. It was Marie Antoinette who banished wide-hoop panniers from her court; in 1926 Coco Chanel introduced the little black dress to women the world over who, before then, primarily wore black when in mourning. In the 1980s, designer Donna Karan transformed women's work wear from manly power suits to feminine separates in body-hugging knits.

The style gyrations rage on. There's more interest in fashion today than ever before, thanks to a media-driven culture, unlimited access, years of prosperity, and the obsession with youth. But buying into fashion isn't the same thing as having style, of course, and American women have always sought guidance in forming their tastes, as fashion is typically a collective concept rather than an individualistic one. There was a time, for many years, when American society women looked to the European aristocracy for style inspiration. But then the glamour of Hollywood took hold and the culture of celebrity was born.

No one would have guessed, at the outset, that movie magic would come to consume the public in the way that it has, but its influence on how women dress made an impact from the moment the first pictures flickered across screens. America embraced its celluloid stars for many years, but that seems to be changing. Stars today, with all of their haute wardrobes, lineless faces, and expensive jewels, are far removed from everyday reality (to say nothing of their other fabricated parts). The Hollywood example has always been in contrast to how real women look and dress, but it's growing more irrelevant by the day. Real women today are more diverse, heavier, curvier, older, and live lives that do not benefit from a team of professional beautifiers. Which is why we, as a country, are devouring the notion of a new style icon.

Michelle Obama is a mature, accomplished woman, a more realistic representation of modern womanhood than any twenty-something starlet could ever hope to be. Yes, her husband is the president of the United States, but possibly Michelle Obama has an equally uncharted job. The role of First Lady is one she must navigate through the scope of impossibly high expectations. If that weren't enough, she has also become the fashion icon that the country has been needing, wanting, *craving* for years. She is the right woman at the right time, a beacon of modern-day flair. Her style has evolved over her lifetime, of course, but it was always clear she took very seriously the way she presented herself to the world.

———————————●———————————

Opposite: Then senator Barack Obama and Michelle, campaigning in Raleigh, North Carolina. As the campaign grew in intensity, Michelle made more and more public appearances, letting the voters get to know her, and her style, slowly.

The Woman and the Clothes

Michelle Obama was born on January 17, 1964, and raised on the South Side of Chicago. Her father, Fraser Robinson, was a pump operator for the Chicago Water Department and a Democratic precinct captain (diagnosed with multiple sclerosis at a young age, he died in 1991). Her mother, Marian, was a Spiegel's secretary who later stayed home to raise Michelle and her older brother, Craig. The Robinson family, by all accounts, enjoyed a warm and supportive home life, one marked by family meals, card games, and animated debate. Barack Obama has joked that, upon meeting the Robinsons, he thought the whole scene very "Leave it to Beaver." Michelle never contested that depiction, and she has said that although hers was not a glamorous upbringing, it was a happy one.

From an early age, Michelle was driven to succeed. She excelled in school, first at Chicago's Bryn Mawr Elementary School and then at Whitney Young High School, Chicago's first magnet high school. Michelle's mother has said that even on the long bus commute to Whitney (ninety minutes each way), Michelle used the time to study, the payoff of which was four years on the honor roll and a place among the members of the

National Honor Society. Michelle went on to Princeton University, where she majored in sociology and minored in African American studies, graduating cum laude in 1985; she obtained a law degree from Harvard University in 1988, and is only the third First Lady to hold a postgraduate degree (following Hillary Clinton and Laura Bush).

Michelle met Barack Obama when she was assigned to mentor him while he was a summer associate at the law firm for which they both worked, Sidley & Austin. Of meeting him, Michelle has said that her reluctance to date someone she worked with was superseded by Barack's wit, generosity, and enthusiasm for causes that they both cared for. They married in Chicago in October 1992.

From the outset, theirs was a marriage built on mutual admiration, and they supported each other in fulfilling the lofty career goals that they each harbored. After her tenure at the Sidley & Austin law firm, Michelle held public sector positions in the

---

Opposite: Barack and Michelle on their wedding day, pictured with Michelle's mother, Marian Robinson (left), and Barack's mother, Ann Dunham (second from right). Michelle's attire for their special day was traditional: a long off-the-shoulder gown with a full veil. Little did she know then that she would become a style icon. **This page, top:** Attending a fund-raising luncheon in Boca Raton, Florida, in her husband's honor, then senator Barack, Michelle opted for a white, sleeveless sheath. The silhouette of that dress would remain a favorite of hers, but the hairstyle, a short "flip," would eventually grow out to a longer length and a decidedly softer shape. **This page, bottom:** Barack and Michelle Obama attend the 36th Annual NAACP Image Awards in Los Angeles, California, March 19, 2005. Michelle is already exhibiting her fondness for sleeveless looks, in a silk satin, printed, strappy gown selected for the occasion.

Chicago city government as an assistant to the mayor, and as the assistant commissioner of planning and development. In 1993 she became the executive director for the Chicago office of Public Allies, a nonprofit organization that recruited young people from all backgrounds to work on social issues. With Barack in Washington, D.C. three days a week in his role as a U.S. senator (he was elected in 2004), Michelle found the dual task of handling the home front and blazing the career trail to be stressful. Like so many women of her time—smart, educated, career driven—after building a family, she found there were hard choices to be made.

In 2002, after years working in the public sector, Michelle was offered the University of Chicago Hospitals position (first as executive director, then as vice president, for community affairs). She has said in interviews that the job was too good to pass up: they offered her flexibility in her schedule, time working from home, and a large salary. But once the demands of Barack's campaign took over, she took a leave of absence from her job.

The Michelle Obama look? It is sleek and streamlined, classic and creative, decidedly American. She experiments with color, embraces comfort, accentuates the positive, and eschews the impractical. She gets it right most of the time, and, like all of us, sometimes gets it wrong. She is a champion of younger, lesser-known designers, such as Jason Wu, Isabel Toledo, and Peter Sorenon, and yet she appreciates the established artistry of Michael Kors and Narciso Rodriguez. She's also sensible enough to shop in well-known chains such as J.Crew

and savvy enough to embrace the new, stylish discounters such as H&M. The Michelle Obama style is uniquely American because it is undeniably modern, with an aesthetic that is both aspirational and accessible at the same time.

For the first time in decades, American women have a style icon who shows us the fun and joy of fashion. Michelle understands the rules and tricks required to wear clothes with individuality. She plays with her look: she knows that dresses can be traditional, or they can be unusual and of varying lengths and necklines; that they can look sleek and polished whether they are patterned, textured, or embellished, or layered with cardigans and topped with coats. She is sure in the knowledge that statement jewelry can change the appearance of anything in an instant, that there's always a place for the classics in any wardrobe, and that versatility is a fashion-lover's best friend. Above all else, Michelle understands intrinsically that style can be a creative endeavor and an artistic expression, and moreover, be something

Opposite, top: Michael Kors, a long-established designer who is considered a master of American sportswear, is one of the few "old guard" fashion insiders that Michelle has worn. His black sheath with slight racer-back armholes was the dress Michelle chose for her official White House portrait. **Opposite, bottom:** Narciso Rodriguez is a designer beloved by celebrities, socialites, and real women alike. Known for his use of luxurious fabrics and simple, streamlined cuts that flatter a woman's shape, he is a master of luxury. Michelle has worn his creations to great effect. **Left:** Ikram Goldman, a Chicago boutique owner, has known Michelle for years. Her taste for sleek and stylish clothes, and her affinity for new, young designers, has suited Michelle's taste as well. Goldman continues to advise the First Lady on matters of fashion.

that smart, modern women enjoy.

Michelle Obama employs a number of staple pieces in her wardrobe. She loves dresses, and who can blame her? At five foot ten she wears them well. And the ease of such one-stop dressing is something to which all busy women can relate. There's been extensive debate over her arms (and her right to bare them!), and even though Jackie Kennedy and Nancy Reagan both wore sleeveless gowns for their husband's inauguration parties, Michelle's arms are statement-making in their own right: strong and powerful, like the woman who flexes them. She likes saturated color, such as purple, teal, and persimmon, and also retro-inspired prints, such as silk shantung covered in rose blooms.

She has been photographed in countless empire waistlines, all the better to accentuate her long, lean frame, to say nothing of the parade of cardigan sweaters she has sported. Her skirts are either sleek and straight (the pencil skirt being a favorite) or full and gathered, and, like many fashion lovers, she lets mood and occasion dictate the time for which. She has perfected the belt—cinching everything from dresses to cardigans to coats—and has catapulted that accessory into the international spotlight. For her first official portrait, Michelle Obama selected a simple, black, sleeveless sheath by American designer Michael Kors, her own nod to how perennially appropriate it is to wear a little black dress. Her jewelry? It makes a statement. Like Jackie Kennedy and the Bush women before her, Michelle has brought pearls back into vogue, but she made them her own by choosing ones

that are big and bold (and, for the record, not real). She also employs heavily jewel-encrusted brooches, oversized hoop earrings, and multistrand necklaces.

Michelle gets a lot of help, of course, and shows us that knowing whom to ask is as important as asking in the first place. Ikram Goldman, a forty-one-year-old Chicago boutique owner, started advising her during the campaign and has continued to guide her. It has been reported that Goldman was responsible for working with Isabel Toledo on Michelle's inauguration ensemble, as well as coordinating many of the choices Michelle wore during the Obamas' first trip abroad in April 2009 (Michelle received high marks for her stylishness on that trip, and it seemed as if the entire world was following her daily wardrobe choices). Goldman has also been instrumental in introducing Michelle to some of the lesser-known designers whose work she has worn, a move that has

Opposite, top left: Michelle's ability to mix designer wear with clothes that are considered reasonably priced has delighted American women who feel she dresses sensibly. Here, heading into the campaign plane wearing a striped dress from retailer H&M, she signals to the press corps that she'll be right back. **Opposite, bottom left:** For her appearance on the ABC television show *The View*, Michelle wore this black and white sheath. The dress, from affordable retailer White House | Black Market, cost $148. In what would become an early indicator of Michelle's influence as a style setter, it has been reported that after the show aired, the dress sold out in a matter of days. **Opposite, right:** Michelle, after meeting with Sarah Brown, wife of British prime minister Gordon Brown, departs wearing a jeweled cardigan and a lime-hued pencil skirt. The ensemble, from retailer J.Crew, became an instant hit, selling out in J.Crew's stores and on its website within days.

irked some (such as Oscar de la Renta, who made some critical comments in an interview he gave to the fashion newspaper *Women's Wear Daily*, which he later retracted) and pleased others. Goldman, known for her impeccable taste, will likely remain a key advisor to Michelle for the foreseeable future.

It is for all these reasons that women look to Michelle Obama with respect and admiration as a style icon of our time. She is serious and sexy, easy and accessible, down-to-earth and beautiful. She is an everywoman on her most pulled-together day. What she has done that none have been able to do before her is be a thinking-woman's fashion muse. She makes us realize that no matter how smart and accomplished you are, it's still okay to get lost in the women's Monday morning quarter-backing of who-wore-what. It is still anyone's guess as to what lasting effect Michelle Obama's fashion legacy will have on the public, but one thing's for sure: today, she matters deeply. She has single-handedly invigorated every woman's idea of what personal style can be.

Opposite, top: Nancy Reagan, dancing with entertainer Frank Sinatra at one of her husband's inaugural balls in 1981. President Reagan, seen trying to "cut in," always supported his wife's interest in fashion. **Opposite, bottom:** At the Democratic National Convention's last night, Michelle had to employ many costume changes during the multiday event. This printed dress was a standout, cleverly accessorized with brooches at the neckline for added sparkle. Her younger daughter, Sasha, rests on her lap. **This page, top:** At the start of the Democratic National Convention in Denver, Michelle took center stage. By now she had become accustomed to her high-visibility role, and she had also evolved her style. Here she wears a sheath in a saturated color, teal, with a bold brooch pinned front and center. **This page, bottom:** Michelle and then candidate Barack Obama arrive for the primary results in Raleigh, North Carolina. Here, Michelle combines many of her style staples: bold color, a sheath with an empire waist, and pearls.

Inauguration Day and Night: She Is the One

O n Inauguration Day alone, it is estimated that, in addition to the millions of people who watched the proceedings while standing on the Washington Mall that frigid January day, and the 37.8 million U.S. television viewers, there were millions tuning in online, from every corner of the globe (in fact, viewers watching the inauguration broke streaming video traffic records for CNN.com, FoxNews.com, and MSNBC.com). When Barack Obama became the forty-fourth president of the United States, it's possible there were more eyeballs on the event then there had been for any other event in history. His swearing in was an historic moment, and the importance of the occasion was lost on no one. Standing by his side on that clear day was Michelle Obama, dressed to reflect all that the new administration wanted to embody: hope, change, and renewal.

There was much speculation as to what Michelle would wear, for both the day and the evening. Would she use a classic American designer with a proven track record of dressing First Ladies? Or would it be an unknown, eager newcomer thrust into the spotlight? Would her day ensemble be a suit, a dress, or some fabulous combination of separates? Many assumed she'd opt for a red evening gown—it being classic, patriotic, and flat-

This page, below: Isabel Toledo, a Cuban-born designer who is based in New York, was reportedly contacted by stylist Ikram Goldman and asked to design a daytime look for the inauguration. Toledo, who envisioned the First Lady as symbolizing renewal, chose a shade she calls lemongrass for the sheath, cardigan, and coat ensemble. **This page, top left:** As both an added layer of color and for warmth, Michelle wore a pair of loden green leather gloves. **This page, top right:** The temperatures were in the teens that day, but for the new president and First Lady, the excitement of the day kept the chill off. **This page, bottom right:** The Obamas, on the morning of the inauguration, looked resplendent. The embellished neckline on Michelle's sheath peeked out and reflected the morning light ever so subtly, and the lemongrass-hued coat, with a ribbon tie and an empire waist, added texture to the look. **Opposite:** Michelle Obama waves to the cheering crowd that lined Pennsylvania Avenue that January morning. Designer Isabel Toledo has said she added an extra lining to the inside of the coat, made of silk, for added warmth.

tering, as well as a color she seemed to favor—but no one knew until the end, including, it would come to light, the designer ultimately chosen for the task.

Isabel Toledo is a forty-eight-year-old Cuban-born designer who is based in New York City. It has been reported that Michelle has been buying the designer's clothes from a shop in Chicago, the Obamas' hometown, for more than twenty years. Toledo met Michelle at a fund-raiser a few months before the inauguration, and the soon-to-be First Lady was interested in the designer's ideas for an inaugural ensemble. Toledo, a smart, hard-working, smaller-scale designer, has said in interviews that she was most impressed with Michelle's warmth and openness upon meeting her, and was eager to capture that spirit in a design. But the pressure of creating something that the First Lady would wear on inauguration day was a daunting task. What would it be, *exactly*? How would it be styled? What would it be made out of? The color? The details? The overall feel of the ensemble? Imagine the challenge she faced trying to incorporate the elements of comfort, ease, and warmth—all integral pieces to the design puzzle.

Toledo went to work sketching ideas. The designer, well adept at creating modern, tailored clothes, is said to have taken her inspiration from the style choices that she had already seen from Michelle, and from her own philosophy that contemporary clothes are classic designs that have an element of surprise. A dress can be just a dress, or it can be transformative, from the use of an interesting, textural fabric, a saturated color, or a sleek silhouette; a coat can be just a coat, or it can make a statement with the clever use of cut, styling, and finishing details. Toledo's design would be sending a message to the world, and above all else she wanted it to *say* something.

In Michelle Obama, Toledo had a dream client: a woman at the prime of her life, at the pinnacle of her family's journey, in what was surely considered a defining moment in the country's history. And for the day, Toledo created a lemongrass-hued ensemble in three parts: a sheath of wool lace that was backed in white silk and embellished at the neckline, a cardigan, and a coordinating coat that was fitted through the torso and tied at the waist with a length of green ribbon. When the weather prediction called for frigid temperatures on the day of the inauguration, the coat got a last-minute additional lining of silk for a discreet (but necessary) layer of warmth. The finishing touches? Michelle Obama added deep green Jimmy Choo kitten-heeled pumps and loden leather gloves from J.Crew.

When the Obamas were first spotted on the morning of the inauguration, Michelle's dress radiated. It fit and flattered, and accentuated her long frame, but by far the profound beauty of that dress was the color: not quite yellow, not quite green. It was rich and saturated and bold, ever so fitting for the event, the woman, and the season. It shimmered ever so subtly in the morning sun, and in one fell swoop it was as if that dress said everything the country was feeling: it's a new day.

After she had hit what can only be described as a fashion home run for the daytime festivities, the anticipation regarding what she'd wear that evening mounted. Let's face it, there was a lot of pressure, but the response was immediate: when her husband noticed (and said aloud, to an eruption of hoots and howls from the audience) at the first of their ten inaugural balls of the evening, "How good looking is my wife?" it was a great moment. This man, the new president of the United States, just wanted to take time to admire his wife. We loved him for that candid admission, and we thought the same thing, yes, she *does* look good.

For this dress, the gown to end all gowns, it has been reported that Michelle considered many designers. Fashion insiders opined that she'd choose something by great American designer Ralph Lauren, or the designer who has dressed so many First Ladies, Oscar de la Renta. In the end, Michelle again chose a designer who was less established but highly respected within the fashion community nonetheless. Taipei-born Jason Wu, twenty-six years old, watched the inauguration in anticipation with the rest of the world. He has said he was enjoying the televised events from his New York City apartment, with a small gathering of close friends. Few people knew he had, in fact, made a gown for

Opposite, top: Michelle accessorized her dress with an armload of faceted bangles, bringing out the silver embroidery in the gown and catching the television lights beautifully. **Opposite, bottom left:** Michelle wore one large cocktail ring. Dancing with her husband, her hand gently resting on his shoulder, the sparkler dazzled. **Opposite, bottom right:** Although Michelle doesn't often wear dangling earrings, on this night she opted for cascading diamonds for added glamour.

Above: Jason Wu, just twenty-six years old when he was asked to design a "special event" gown for Michelle, had no idea that his creation would be chosen for the big night. He has said in interviews that he was watching the night's festivities on television and was flabbergasted when Michelle took the stage in his design. **This page, right:** The dress that went around the world: Michelle wearing an original design by Jason Wu. The world seemed to wait in anticipation of what she would choose that night. Many thought she'd make her selection for an older, more-established designer, but Michelle chose the twenty-six-year-old Wu instead. The move shocked some, but it reflected the First Lady's interest in championing lesser-known talent. **Opposite:** The First Couple, dancing their first dance with a serenade by the singer Beyoncé, who crooned the song that both Glen Miller and Etta James made famous, "At Last."

the First Lady, and nobody knew if it would ever be worn, let alone worn that night. In the myriad of interviews that came later, Wu said he was only told he was making a gown for a special event, and that he had never even met Michelle Obama. At the moment the world saw it, Wu saw it, and the designer was positively awestruck.

The gown, never actually fitted on the First Lady, was made of creamy-white layers of silk chiffon, and embellished with organza, Swarovski crystal rhinestones, and silver thread embroidery. Its Grecian styling, with a high waist and a gathering of fabric that looped over one shoulder, was regal and ethereal, and seemed to sway and float independently. In this dress, Michelle was the star of her own fairy tale, and of the country's suspended reality as well. The dress was quiet in its own way, devoid of elaborate, heavy beading, but it spoke volumes. The color, long associated with purity, was not in this case wedding-like at all. Although critics are torn on matters of fit and whether the styling and fabrication worked best on Michelle's frame, the conclusion is that the overall effect was luminous, giving her sophisticated, grown-up appeal. It was clean, airy, diaphanous. Not quite sexy but decidedly sensual, it portrayed the casual elegance that the public was coming to recognize as a hallmark of this First Lady.

Previous First Ladies made other fashion choices, of course, and all of them were, in one way or another, indicative of the times and emblematic of the women who wore them. For her husband's inaugural in 1961, Jackie Kennedy wore a long, sleeveless column made of off-white chiffon, accessorized with long white gloves and worn with a white cape over the top The look was in sharp contrast to the full-skirted 1950s styling that women were used to seeing, and it accentuated Jackie Kennedy's lean frame and formal posture. In 1965 Lady Bird Johnson opted for a simple pale yellow gown in double-weave silk, but the critics were harsh (not chic, they cried). Pat Nixon faced her own fashion challenges when it was her time: the current popularity of hippie styling was in sharp contrast to her husband's conservative politics. Feeling it her duty to represent her husband's administration, she chose a gold and silver gown made of mimosa silk satin, which ended up looking miserably old-fashioned and out of step with the times.

Roslyn Carter decided to shop her own closet: She pulled out a blue chiffon gown with gold trim that she had worn six years earlier when her husband became governor of Georgia. The choice spoke volumes, for the woman *and* the administration, to the fact that the country, recovering from one oil embargo and soon to face another, was facing cost-conscious times. Naturally, when the Reagans arrived in 1981, the country braced itself for Hollywood glamour. Nancy's choice? A white, one-shouldered, lace, silk satin sheath with crystal

---

Opposite: John Kennedy, the thirty-fifth president of the United States, and his wife, Jackie, arrive at the National Guard Armory for their inaugural ball. Jackie, who wore an off-white sleeveless column gown, layered a white cape over the top for warmth.

and bugle beads by the designer James Galanos. It cost a reported $10,000, and, given that the country was on the brink of a recession, seemed to some to reflect a tin ear. For Reagan's reelection in 1985, Nancy wore another white gown, this one of chiffon and heavily beaded, and still far from frugal: reports that Reagan tallied up an inaugural wardrobe that totaled $46,000 outraged the public.

Barbara Bush wore royal blue lace and velvet by the designer Arnold Scaasi; Hillary Clinton wore a violet creation of lace and velvet in many layers, by Sarah Phillips, a designer unknown to most of the public, which was universally loathed as looking theatrical and heavy handed. She did better the second time around, opting for a sleek Oscar de la Renta gown of gold embroidery. Some even called it sexy. Laura Bush chose a red Chantilly lace gown with beading and embroidery designed by Oscar de la Renta for her husband's first inaugural in 2001, and a pale blue and silver embroidered V-neck gown, also by Oscar de la Renta, for her husband's reelection in 2005.

Every First Lady is faced with the challenge of accepting the public's perception of who they are based on how they dress. It's not something any man, in any field, has to contend with. But women the world over know it to be true. One of the most endearing qualities about Michelle Obama is that, by her own admission, her goal is to be the most authentic version of herself that she can possibly be. You see it in all areas of her life—such as the fact that she kept her job longer than anyone would have imagined she would, or that she always puts her children first before committing to appearances—and the way she dresses is a prime example of that sensibility. She wears what she likes (designed by who she likes), she wears what works on her body, and she wears what feels right. She does it in her own way and with her own flair, and that, in turn, is what genuine personal style is all about.

Opposite, left: For her husband's first inaugural celebration in 2001, Laura Bush chose a red Chantilly lace gown with beading and embroidery, made for her by designer Oscar de la Renta. The style may have been termed conservative by some, but the color "popped" on camera, and, of course, looked very patriotic. **Opposite, right:** For her husband's second inaugural, in 2005, Laura Bush selected a pale blue and silver embroidered gown by designer Oscar de la Renta. The dress, more form fitting and sinuous than many of her previous looks, garnered high marks from the fashion press.

Michelle:
A Gallery of Photographs

Empire sheaths in bold hues…sleeveless evening wear in form-fitting silhouettes…breezy shirtdresses in feminine floral prints…colorful cardigans…strands of pearls. These are the new buzz phrases floating in and out of stores and design houses, and on the pages devoted to fashion news and commentary. Call it the Michelle Effect.

A lot has been said about our First Lady's sense of style. Her look is not only her own, it is a departure. In a relatively short time, Michelle has said so long to the sensible heels, pale pantyhose, and boxy suits of yesteryear, and she has given a hearty welcome to a world of smart flats, bare legs and arms, and softer separates. Her chic modernity comes not only from her choices, but as a result of her dressing with the authenticity of a woman who knows who she is. It's called personal style. What's that, exactly? It's being clever enough to know which clothes work best for you, confident enough to be creative, contemporary enough to break old rules, and sensible enough to ignore critics. In other words, personal style is not what you wear but rather how you wear it, and by all accounts Michelle Obama has it.

The public fascination isn't likely to abate. Women the world over are delighted to have such a modern muse—finally, a woman in the White House who dresses like the intelligent, savvy, multitasking mother/wife/professional that she is. So the next time you're in a restaurant, or at the mall, or standing in line at the checkout, and the woman next to you is wearing a belted cardigan, or a long coat over a pair of slim capri pants, or a sleeveless dress in a shock of color, you may very well chalk it up to the Michelle Effect.

This page, right: In a photo taken before Michelle and Barack were married, Michelle sits in front the humble stone-built house belonging to Barack's stepmother, Kezia. It was reported that years later, Kezia watched the U.S. presidential election results on an old television set, just inside. **This page, below left:** Although Michelle was a serious student from a young age, no one would have known then that she was destined for such great things. She's pictured here prior to her discovery of sleeveless sheaths in bold colors, but she sure is cute! **This page, below right:** Michelle Robinson at her undergraduate graduation from Princeton University. **Opposite, top left:** When they were still dating, Barack and Michelle celebrated Christmas in Hawaii. **Opposite, top right:** In 1996 the Obamas traveled to England to see the country and also attend Barack's half sister Auma's wedding. Here, Barack's stepmother, Kezia (seated, left) and his half sister, Maya Soetoro (standing), are pictured with Michelle (seated, right).
Opposite, bottom: An intimate family photo from the Obama wedding album: L to R: Marian Robinson (Michelle's mother), Michelle, and Auma Obama (Barack's half sister).

This page, right: Leave it to Michelle to put a twist on a classic color (red) as well as a traditional piece (jacket). This one, with its exaggerated collar, provides a dramatic frame for her face. **Below:** Early in the campaign, Michelle's look was more corporate executive, including her then signature "flip" hairstyle. Here, in a classic white blouse with rolled collar, she met with a group of working women in Stanford, Connecticut, to discuss the commitment that her husband's administration will have to issues that affect working families. **Opposite, left:** Michelle listens as her Democratic-hopeful husband speaks to residents of Oskaloosa, Iowa, during an Independence Day celebration. Casually dressed in a black skirt and white tank, her flip hairstyle was soon replaced by something softer and longer. **Opposite, top right:** Early in the campaign, Michelle's style was not quite as evolved. Her penchant for pearls, however, is already on display in this 2007 photo, taken at a campaign rally on the campus of the University of Illinois during a three-day presidential announcement trip. **Opposite, bottom right:** Michelle turns a pinstripe shirt on its side. Here, greeting the staff at the San Jorge Children's Hospital in San Juan, Puerto Rico, she transforms a classic shell. This one, a face-framing winner, may have soft folds of fabric but it still looks crisp.

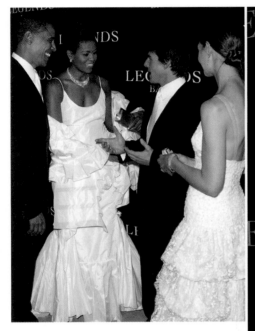

This page, right: Then senator Obama and Michelle arrive at the Legends Ball, an award ceremony hosted by Oprah Winfrey, honoring women who have paved the way in the arts, entertainment, and civil rights. All women were asked to wear white, and Michelle was no exception. In this spaghetti-strapped gown and silk, ruffled "cardigan," she dazzled. **Above:** Michelle and Barack greet Tom Cruise and Katie Holmes. Michelle accessorized her gown with white's perfect pairing: diamonds. **Opposite, top left:** Looking every bit like a family destined for the White House, the Obamas pose for a portrait at their home in Chicago in 2004. Michelle's now trademark pearls were an essential from the start. **Opposite, top right:** In 2004, Barack was a Democratic nominee from Illinois for the U.S. Senate. Pictured here with Michelle and their daughters, Sasha, left, and Malia, right, the family awaits election returns in a Chicago hotel. Michelle, already exhibiting her taste for unusual colors, wears a suit in a color that looks for all the world to be lemongrass. Perhaps it was a fashion foreshadow to the ensemble she wore on the day of Barack's presidential inauguration. **Opposite, bottom:** In this 2005 photo, then vice president Dick Cheney administers the Senate Oath to Barack during a mock swearing-in on Capitol Hill. Michelle has evolved her look since then into something considerably more casual and more youthful.

SLEEVELESS SILHOUETTES

Michelle Obama is not the first First Lady to go sleeveless, nor is she the first to ignite a debate regarding the style. Both Jackie Kennedy and Nancy Reagan wore sleeveless dresses at one time or another, and in fact both of them went sleeveless for their husband's inaugural galas—Jackie in 1961 and Nancy for her husband's first inaugural in 1981. The former was deemed too risqué when she did it, and the latter was accused of flaunting her Hollywood glamour when she did (for her husband's second inaugural celebration, Nancy Reagan wore sleeves, it should be noted). But whatever the press may or may not have thought at the time, history has served both women well: their sleeveless looks are now thought to have been ahead of the fashion curve. Michelle's love of the style seems more abiding—she's devoted to the look—and she favors it more than any of her predecessors. Everyone's talking about her arms—glamorous, strong, and athletic—giving her look an unmistakable message of modern confidence. What makes it such a style statement is that she's going sleeveless all year around. Called "seasonless dressing," this style is a buzz phrase within the fashion community and a strong trend for the way modern women dress.

Opposite, top: On the final day of the Democratic National Convention, Michelle makes her way through the crowd at Invesco Field in Denver. Her black sleeveless sheath is set off with a bold brooch pinned at the center of the V-neck. Statement jewelry is another Michelle hallmark. **Opposite, middle:** With candidate Barack about to become the Democratic nominee, Michelle accompanies her husband at the convention. Here she exhibits a perfect example of her evolving style: a sleeveless dress in a vibrant color, belted at the waist. The American public would come to see this look as a hallmark of the Michelle Obama sensibility. **Opposite, bottom left:** For the president's first address to a joint session of Congress at the Capitol in Washington, D.C., Michelle chose to go sleeveless in a deep eggplant–hued creation by designer Narciso Rodriguez. **Opposite, bottom right:** As the campaign became more intense, Michelle made many more appearances. Here, for her taping of the popular Comedy Central show *The Colbert Report*, she selected a bold (and patriotic) blue sleeveless dress. **This page, left:** Michelle makes a departure from her usual sleek sheaths in this full-skirted plaid dress. The occasion? A bicentennial celebration for former president Abraham Lincoln at Ford's Theater's grand reopening in Washington, D.C. **Above:** Wearing a taupe sleeveless shell and accessorized with three bold strands of beads, Michelle listens during an economic roundtable for women in August 2008.

Opposite, top left: During the presidential campaign, Michelle often spoke to women's groups around the country. Here she addresses a group at the New York Historical Society's Women in Public Life benefit luncheon in July 2007. Michelle's early look, like this, was that of a corporate executive. Over the course of the campaign she evolved to having one that was more accessible and more creative. **Opposite, top right:** In March 2007, Michelle took daughters, Malia, top, and Sasha, bottom, to Disneyland. Here, in front of Sleeping Beauty's castle, Michelle's relaxed ease makes her look like every other adoring mom. **Opposite, below:** The Obama family, celebrating Barack's senatorial win on Election Night 2004, are lost in a blizzard of confetti. **This page, left:** Michelle on the campaign trail in Windham, New Hampshire, in May 2007. Her style? Accessible casual chic, in a color that flatters her. **Below, left:** Michelle campaigns on behalf of her husband in June 2007 in Council Bluffs, Iowa. What better way to shake up a gray pencil skirt? A shock of color. Here, Michelle's bright coral sleeveless shell is perfect, and it also reflects a lovely glow onto her face. **Below, right:** Michelle is seen here in June 2007 addressing female community members at the Cambridge Community Center in Las Vegas. In a sheer top with inlaid ribbon detailing, she shows us she's not averse to showing her girly side.

Opposite: At a February 2008 rally in Los Angeles, California, Michelle channels West Coast casual chic. Here, she stands tall with a few very accomplished women, Caroline Kennedy, Maria Shriver, and Oprah Winfrey. **This page, top:** Michelle and Barack, early on the campaign trail. Michelle may not have yet given up her "flip" hairstyle, but she's already embracing bold color. **This page, bottom:** How best to wear polka dots? Just like this. Keep the background black and the dots small in size, and rein in volume with a belted waist. And, proving that details matter, the flared sleeve is a lovely feminine touch.

Opposite: A quiet moment before the final election storm: while on the campaign trail, Michelle and Barack enjoy dinner out at Jorge's Sombrero Mexican restaurant in Pueblo, Colorado. **This page, left:** Michelle and her younger daughter, Sasha, wait on the tarmac for then Democratic presidential candidate Barack to step off the plane. Even on her most dressed-down days, Michelle embraces saturated color. **This page, top right:** Michelle and Barack, then a presidential hopeful, greet the crowd during his primary night rally in Nashua, New Hampshire. This look from Michelle is more old than new: the turtlenecks and covered legs soon disappeared, and the bright colors and bare legs became important elements of her personal style. **This page, bottom right:** In the audience for a speech Barack delivered at the Apostolic Church of God in Chicago in June 2008, Michelle stands with her daughters, looking relaxed. This empire-waisted white dress exudes casual comfort.

Above: While campaigning in Atlantic, Iowa, the Obamas take a moment for a warm embrace. That they were surrounded by onlookers and photographers didn't seem to bother them at all. **This page, right:** Pictured with Oprah Winfrey while on the campaign trail, Michelle wears a long coat that would work in an office but that's far from business as usual. Its subtle texture and design, coupled with a soft shape and bell sleeves, looks luxe. **Opposite, left:** At a campaign stop in Berlin, New Hampshire, in May 2007, Barack seems pleased as punch to be introduced by his wife.

Opposite, top right: Quintessential Michelle: A sleeveless, sleek sheath in a shock of color, with a brooch pinned to one shoulder. Here on the campaign trail, Michelle heads to the podium to speak at a Women for Obama luncheon in Chicago.

Opposite, bottom right: Michelle's penchant for mixing high-end designers with "regular" clothes is a first for a First Lady. While attending a rally on the campaign trail, she wears a striped, sleeveless dress from lower-priced retailer H&M.

THE PANACHE OF COLOR AND PATTERN

It takes a confident woman to wear bold colors, and Michelle Obama wears them often. For starters, she veers away from the traditional red, navy, and green, and instead favors "off" colors, such as teal, burgundy, and purple, which require an artistic appreciation. When the Obamas made their first postelection visit to the White House, Michelle dazzled in an Isabel Toledo dress in a hue that was somewhere on the red-orange spectrum but not quite either color. Certainly her lemongrass inauguration daywear, another Isabel Toledo design, was equally striking. As for pattern, she gravitates toward the unexpected and the bold, unafraid to experiment. Whether it's a fuchsia and black Thakoon-designed dress and topcoat, or a bold argyle sweater by designer Junya Watanabe, Michelle chooses colors and patterns that flatter her face, surprise the eye, and enhance the design of whatever it is she wears.

Opposite, bottom left: In a departure from the structured sheaths that Michelle favored throughout the campaign, she selected something much softer and more romantic for an evening gala in tribute to singer Stevie Wonder in February 2009. The dress, designed by Wonder's wife, Kai Milla, was a standout in vibrant green. Michelle's hair, tousled curls, was another surprise and the ideal accessory. **Opposite, top right:** Michelle learned early on that vibrant color not only flatters her skin tone but also photographs well. In this age, when the role of television has such an enormous effect on the public's perception of a candidate and his message, being telegenic is tantamount. Here, Barack and Michelle arrive for the primary results in Raleigh, North Carolina, a state that Obama would eventually win. **Opposite, bottom right:** Michelle often chooses hues that are considered non-traditional or "off tones." It takes practice, and a keen eye, and Michelle almost always gets it right. Here, standing before cheering supporters, Michelle sports a sheath in vibrant teal. **This page, above left:** On Day 4 of the Democratic National Convention, being held in Denver, Colorado, in August 2008, the Obamas' two young daughters joined their parents for the festivities. Michelle's short puffed-sleeve printed dress was sweet but chic. The proportions were perfect: the skirt, with a bit of volume, perfectly balanced the top. **Above right:** Once Senator Joe Biden was named on the Obama ticket, his wife, Jill, also became a part of the campaign. She and Michelle, both moms with big careers, by all accounts have great respect and admiration for each other. Here, in a more casual moment, Michelle is seen in a breezy, floral-patterned shirtdress with full skirt and self-belt. The mélange of yellows and purples were particularly flattering. **This page, bottom left:** The occasion was the first debate between the two presidential hopefuls, Barack Obama and John McCain. Taking place at the University of Mississippi, the televised event was expected to garner a large audience. Michelle chose a fitted printed sheath, with a black bow accent on one shoulder, which fell just below the knee. The length, which looks retro to some, is one that many designers consider most flattering on a women's leg.

Opposite, top left: Michelle is seen here speaking at a roundtable discussion with military spouses at Old Dominion University in Norfolk, Virginia. The First Lady has said that the obstacles faced by military families is one of the causes she most wants to champion. **Opposite, top center:** At a campaign event in December 2008, a large crowd had gathered at the U.S. Cellular Center in Cedar Rapids, Iowa. It didn't hurt that superstar Oprah Winfrey had joined the Obamas on the trail. Looking superchic in belted black, Michelle revs everyone up. **Opposite, top right:** Appearing at a campaign event in Seattle, Washington, Michelle elevates a white suit out of the realm of ordinary by choosing one with delicate black detailing. The small, rounded collar is a lovely feminine touch. **Opposite, below:** The Obama family arrives at Columbus airport in Ohio while on the campaign trail. Again, Michelle's love of bold, unexpected color is unique to her style. Here, a yellow cardigan is paired with cobalt blue jeans. **This page, left:** While in New York City to attend the "Obama for America" fund-raiser in June 2008, Michelle goes for high style in all black. **Below:** Michelle, speaking at a working women's roundtable discussion at the Crofoot Ballroom in Pontiac, Michigan. Many women recoil at the thought of baring their arms in sleeveless dresses or blouses, but not Michelle. Her well-toned arms are stunning.

ECONOMIC
SECURITY
FOR AMERICAN FAMILIES
WWW.BARACKOBAMA.COM

This page, top right: During the campaign, the Obama girls occasionally attended events with their parents, such as this one in Las Vegas. Michelle's casual attire often features her favorite weekend pant, something slim in a cropped leg, which is always worn with skimmer flats. **Below:** Michelle, attending an economic roundtable for women while in Denver in August of 2008, looks happy and relaxed. The three bold strands around her neck add texture and provide the perfect frame for her face. **This page, below right:** At a Super Tuesday primary rally in February 2008, Michelle smartly opted for a classic red sheath and a coordinating jacket with a puffed-sleeve detail. **Opposite, left:** At the Get Out the Vote rally in Los Angeles, Michelle is all ease and modern sophistication, and the crowd loved every minute. **Opposite, top right:** Michelle walks onto the stage to join her husband after a presidential debate at the University of Mississippi in Oxford, Mississippi in September 2008. Many tall women shy away from bold prints, but not Michelle. She knows that when the pattern is dense and the colors blend, the look is extremely flattering. **Opposite, bottom right:** This floral, short-sleeved dress had a decidedly vintage appeal. Although Michelle embraces solid colors in bright hues, she also enjoys pattern and print, often opting for florals.

CARDIGAN SWEATERS

Cardigans are not just for toddlers and uniformed schoolgirls, it should be made perfectly clear. Michelle Obama uses the sweater to great effect: as an alternative to a sometimes too-formal looking suit jacket—more comfortable than a coat, more complete than a blouse alone. She has made cardigans her own style statement, an easy-to-wear, deconstructed element that can look as pulled together as any jacket. It is an inherently versatile piece, and Michelle wears the sweater in all colors and incarnations (basic black, boldly colored, embellished, and even asymmetrical). They are fitted, sometimes belted, often adorned with a brooch, always sleek. Above all else, they are totally premeditated and intentional pieces of an overall effect, not a last-minute outer layer as most women wear them.

Opposite, left: During their first European tour since Barack took office, Michelle's every fashion choice was on display and beamed around the world. A media circus, some called it, but Michelle maintained her usual calm reserve. This cardigan, an asymmetrical argyle by designer Junya Watanabe, seemed too edgy for some. Regardless, it made a statement, and fashion insiders raved. **Opposite, right:** For an evening event during the Obamas' first European tour in the spring of 2009, Michelle arrived wearing a black Azzedine Alaia dress with a fitted bodice. On top, a shrunken black cardigan, almost shruglike, kept the evening chill off her shoulders. The play on proportion was a great effect: the miniature sweater balancing the full, layered skirt. **This page, left:** While in Britain on the Obama's European tour, spring 2009, Michelle and Sarah Brown (not pictured), wife of British prime minister Gordon Brown, visit Maggie's Cancer Caring Centre in west London. For the occasion, Michelle donned a slim, pale, lime green pencil skirt and a cream, jeweled cardigan nipped at the waist. A crisp day look, the ensemble came from retailer J.Crew. **Below:** Michelle's life as a First Lady often seems like a whirlwind of events and the logistics that go along with them. Traveling is a part of the job, of course, but there are perks, such as having private transportation. Here, in a casual moment while deplaning with her family, Michelle wears one of her beloved cardigans. This one, loose and longer, is a flattering style over her cropped cigarette pants.

Opposite, top left: The Obamas attended a campaign rally in Bicentennial Park in Miami, Florida, in October 2008. Who says pleats are hard to wear? As Michelle shows us, when the look is kept simple (and monochromatic) and the color dark, it can be incredibly feminine as well as flattering. Soon after this picture was taken, her husband announced he would suspend his campaign so that he could visit his ailing grandmother in Hawaii. **Opposite, bottom left:** There is a distinct amiability factor with Michelle: people like her. Whether she's addressing a crowd of thousands or a room of a few, the First Lady's charisma is only matched by her warmth. It's one of the many things that endears her to the American public. **Opposite, right:** What's the best way to liven up a pale slate hue? Dress in layers to add dimension, and accessorize with something subtle. Here, Michelle uses an offset brooch to pull everything together. **This page, left:** Michelle stands on the stage of the Democratic National Convention with her daughters, Sasha, left, and Malia, right, as they tour the site in preparation for her speech that night. Wearing a pea green jacket with tailored black pants, Michelle makes a winning play on proportion: a short, cropped top over a long bottom looks modern. **Below:** President-elect Barack and Michelle take their daughters, Malia, left, and Sasha, right, for a roll around the rink at Great Skates Fun Center in Lafayette, Indiana. The grown-ups? They'll just walk, thanks.

Above: Her long pearls, broken up by colorful flowers, is the perfect pop of something unexpected. **Center:** Michelle and Cindy McCain join their husbands onstage prior to the presidential debate held at Hofstra University. While Cindy opts for a classic cut in a traditional color, Michelle displays her modern take on fashion with long, fitted sheath in periwinkle. Although Michelle and Cindy McCain are at opposite ends of the fashion spectrum, they do both share an affinity for bold color. **Opposite, top:** Then presidential candidate Barack Obama arrives with Michelle to speak at a primary night rally in Saint Paul, Minnesota. Here, Michelle wears a vibrant magenta sheath with her signature chunky black belt. **Opposite, middle:** Michelle and Barack arrive at his South Dakota and Montana presidential primary election night rally in Saint Paul, Minnesota. This sleeveless sheath is the epitome of a modern approach to dressing. The belt, worn as an accent, creates the illusion of an empire waist, a silhouette that's particularly flattering on Michelle. **Opposite, bottom:** The famous "fist bump" delighted onlookers at the primary election night rally in Saint Paul, Minnesota. Critics carped that it was some sort of terrorist gesture, but voters saw it as what it was: a symbol of the Obamas' total partnership and support of each other.

Opposite: Michelle and her daughters, Malia, left, and Sasha, right, wave to the audience at the Democratic National Convention in Denver after Michelle's speech. This is a signature look for Michelle: a sheath with an empire waist in a rich, teal hue, accessorized with a bold brooch pinned front and center. **This page, top left:** Michelle and her daughters, Malia, left, and Sasha, right, greet Barack after he accepts the Democratic presidential nomination. **This page, bottom left:** Michelle and Barack are color-coordinated and complementary, but not overly matching. They look unified. **This page, bottom right:** Michelle walks with her family after her husband's acceptance speech. Her dress, a sheath in an abstract pattern of black, red, and fuchsia, "popped" on camera. **Above:** The First Family rocks casual elegance at a rally at the Cleveland Mall with Bruce Springsteen, left, in November 2008.

A PEARL NECKLACE

Considered a classic, the iridescent orbs have draped necks around the world for hundreds of years. Pearls have long been the status symbol of fashionable women (a testament to their enduring value: in 1916 jeweler Jacques Cartier is said to have purchased the six-story Renaissance mansion that would become his landmark store on New York City's famous Fifth Avenue by trading two pearl necklaces for the valuable property). Today, pearls are for everyone—the only accessory a woman can wear confidently from her fifth birthday party to her fiftieth wedding anniversary—and are still fashionable after all these years. Jackie Kennedy made a double strand famous and ubiquitous, and even now, more than forty-five years after she was First Lady, the "Jackie pearls" are available for sale online on more than two dozen websites. Barbara Bush wore pearls—huge gumball-size ones, and so did her daughter-in-law Laura. Why so popular? Pearls enjoy a certain status, and are instantly recognized as chic and tasteful. Michelle Obama has been wearing pearls since she first appeared on the national stage, and she does so with her own flair. There's an inherent duality to her style—she likes the traditional, but she also likes to experiment—and she uses pearls as the classic "anchor" to her wardrobe, a signature that she wears day or night, for occasions as relaxed as a morning meet-and-greet to as dressed up as a formal affair.

Opposite, top: For her appearance on the popular *The Daily Show with Jon Stewart* on Comedy Central, Michelle chose a tailored blue suit that was set off by a double strand. **Opposite, bottom left:** A close-up of Michelle and the double strand she seems to like so much. Here, arriving for a dinner in London at 10 Downing Street with England's prime minister during the Obamas' first trip abroad since Barack became president, May 2009. **Opposite, bottom right:** President Obama and Michelle leaving Washington's St. John's Episcopal Church following Easter Sunday services in April 2009. Michelle greets the spring day in a printed dress and her favorite pearls. **This page, top left:** Barbara Bush, seen here with Richard Nixon, was never a fashion icon, but she was known for age-appropriate conservative looks. She favored the color blue and wore it frequently, but her signature was her gumball-size pearls, which she wore in either a single or a double strand around her neck. **Above:** Jacqueline Kennedy epitomized taste and style, and her years in the White House were marked by her terrific fashion sense. She made a double strand of pearls the accessory of choice for American women. **Left:** Pearls have been worn by other First Ladies, of course, but not since Barbara Bush donned them have they been worn as much. Whether dressed up or dressed down, Michelle Obama seems to like the bright white orbs.

Above: Michelle is seen here on the second night of the Democratic National Convention with the Bidens. It has been reported widely that Michelle shares a very warm relationship with Jill Biden, an accomplished English professor. **This page, right:** Michelle knows how to wear white: it's best in a simple silhouette with a bit of textural detail. This sheath is perfect on her. Michelle is seen here talking to then VP candidate Joe Biden. **Opposite, left:** Arriving for the primary results in Raleigh, North Carolina, Michelle wore a bright orange sheath. A bold color for a big night. **Opposite, top right:** Then candidate Barack and Michelle wave to the crowd of supporters. With her fashion sense more evolved, she wears many of her signature style elements: bold color, pearls, and bare legs. This orange dress, a departure from First Lady classic colors such as red and cobalt, is a standout. **Opposite, bottom right:** Proving that a little black dress is always chic and always slimming, Michelle shines at an election night rally in San Antonio, Texas.

Opposite: Michelle and Barack greet the cheering crowds gathered at the Lincoln Memorial during the inaugural opening ceremonies. Her camel coat and pencil skirt with a black top and accessories is a quintessential American look.

This page, top: Here, Michelle wears a new take on a little black dress. This one, by designer Narciso Rodriguez, is made with a shock of red and a banded waist-defining "wrapped" midsection. She greets the enormous crowd, standing beside her husband after he delivers his victory speech at his Election Night party at Grant Park, in Chicago.

This page, bottom: The entire family looks pulled-together and full of good cheer as they wave to the crowd.

EMPIRE WAIST

Dating from early Greco-Roman art, the empire waist became popular among European aristocracy during the Napoleonic era, and enjoyed something of a revival in this country in the 1960s. Setting the historical lineage of the design aside, Michelle Obama wears the empire waist because it flatters her frame and presents an unexpected visual effect. The style is an ideal silhouette for so many women because it makes the most of a woman's proportions: The top shows off the torso (often the most delicate part of the body) and the bottom camouflages the lower half, which can be heavier. It is a look that has come in and out of fashion over the years, and Michelle employs an empire waist with regularity. Her most famous example of the design was her Jason Wu–created inauguration gown: A classic empire, it was draped over one shoulder and cinched just above her rib cage, letting the bulk of the gown fall to the ground for a romantic "floaty" effect.

Above: A closer look at Michelle's Jason Wu–designed inaugural gown, exhibiting a classic empire waist. It fit, it flattered, and most importantly, it floated. The subtle train added to the glamour of the look. **Center:** After Barack Obama won the White House, but before he and his family took residence, he and Michelle made the customary visit to the outgoing president. For the occasion, which was a clear, crisp Washington day, Michelle selected an empire-waisted sheath, this time in a vibrant hue somewhere in the spectrum of red and orange. This dress, from favorite designer Maria Pinto, gave her the appearance of an impossibly long frame. **Opposite, top right:** Michelle has certainly developed her strong sense of style over the many years she has been in the public eye, first as wife to then senator Barack Obama, and now as First Lady. In that time she learned what works, and employs certain winning colors, styles, and silhouettes, whether she's dressing for day or night. Here, for a rally while on the campaign trail, Michelle chose a simple white shirt. The twist, of course, is its empire waist, providing a new take on this classic piece. **Opposite, bottom right:** While in Europe with her husband for the First Couple's maiden trip abroad, Michelle dazzled in this empire-waisted sheath with short sleeves. The dress, fashioned out of fuschia silk and covered with black blooms, was topped with a coordinating coat: an incredibly complete, pulled together look that could go from day to night.

This page, top: Michelle arrives for the inauguration ceremony at the U.S. Capitol in Washington. The color of her Isabel Toledo ensemble appeared to shift and change all day, leading some observers wondering what, exactly, to call the shade. **This page, bottom:** Michelle's loden green gloves provided a lovely accent, and visual anchor, to her lemongrass coat and sheath. When pairing accessories, it's best to go darker in tone rather than lighter. **Opposite:** Michelle watches as her younger daughter Sasha gives her father the thumbs up following his taking the oath of office as the 44th president. Michelle chose her color scheme carefully that day, and went with a modern and sophisticated hue. Her girls, on the other hand, wore colors with pop.

Opposite: A private moment on possibly the most public night of their lives. Michelle and Barack enjoy their first dance. **This page, left:** The dress the world waited for: Michelle's inaugural gown. Created by twenty-six-year-old designer Jason Wu, the Grecian-styled dress was made from many layers of cream chiffon and embroidered with silver thread. The empire waistline is a style Michelle wears often, and it accents her long, lean frame beautifully. **Above:** Michelle and Barack dance at the Commander-in-Chief Inaugural Ball at the National Building Museum in Washington. Her dress, with its subtle train, has all the glamour befitting a First Lady.

THE HIGH/LOW COMBINATION

The luxury of putting on a gorgeous, well-made designer dress cannot be underestimated, and Michelle Obama has wisely chosen many wonderful creations to wear. But what makes her choices unique, so smart, and so emblematic of the way real women approach dressing is that she combines designer wear with off-the-rack pieces from some of the country's mass market retailers. Michelle makes everything look great: whether she's wearing a sundress from the Gap that she donned for a Fourth of July parade, or the printed sheath from fashion house White House | Black Market that she wore for a now-famous appearance on the television show *The View*. Funnily enough, it was that event that catapulted Michelle into the fashion spotlight: her dress sold out across the country overnight, and the influence that her choice had on consumers ignited comparisons between her and Jackie Kennedy. Amazing, the power of a $148 dress! And this is exactly what personal style is all about: making choices and mixing it up. It's also what endears Michelle Obama to women the world over. She's a practical, smart shopper and a fashionista of the people.

Opposite, bottom left: There were many inaugural celebrations, and Michelle said in interviews that although she enjoyed them all, the one she found most fun was the Kids' Inaugural: We Are the Future concert. Appearing with her daughters, who thoroughly enjoyed music from the popular Jonas Brothers, Michelle dressed from what was becoming one of her go-to sources, J.Crew. **Opposite, top right:** While visiting with Sarah Brown, wife of British prime minister Gordon Brown, Michelle looked chic in her lime green pencil skirt and cream, jeweled cardigan. Rave reviews ensued, especially when people learned the ensemble came from retailer J.Crew. Naturally, the pieces that made up the "Michelle look" sold out in days, according to reports. **Opposite, middle right:** In the beginning of the campaign, Michelle chose carefully which events and media opportunities she would partake of. But as the months of campaigning wore on, Michelle became much more involved. For her appearance on *The Tonight Show with Jay Leno*, she selected another ensemble from popular retailer J.Crew. The separates, in a range of vibrant yellows, looked great. **Opposite, bottom right:** When Michelle appeared in this striped dress, it took fashion insiders a moment to figure out where it came from. Was it created by designer Michael Kors, master of American sportswear? Perhaps it was from Tory Burch, popular for her classics with a twist? Nope. The crisp sleeveless design came from none other than hip and inexpensive retailer H&M. **This page, left:** On the occasion of the Fourth of July , the nation's birthday, the Obama family enjoyed a parade and the ensuing festivities for a decidedly casual day. Michelle, pictured running with her two girls, is wearing a black-and-white plaid sundress topped with a cardigan. People loved that she looked so youthful; the fashion press was surprised and delighted to learn that the dress came from the Gap.

Above: First Lady Laura Bush gave Michelle a private tour of the artwork in the East Wing of the White House in January 2009, and Michelle looks perfect for the occasion. **This page, bottom right:** The Obamas are pictured helping their daughters get ready to attend their first day at Sidwell Friends School, in Washington, D.C., January 2009. **Opposite, top left:** Michelle arrives in Wilmington, Delaware, on her husband's whistle-stop train trip to Washington, D.C., in January 2009, looking quintessentially modern-day chic in a deep purple coat by designer Maria Cornejo. **Opposite, top right:** Michelle, walking with her elder daughter, Malia, as they return from a weekend at Camp David. Proving her uncanny ability to make weekend attire look stylishly pulled together, Michelle wears a colorful coat in a great shape (notice the slight "bubble" on the lower half). **Opposite, bottom:** On their first day as residents of the White House, the Obamas held an open house reception. Here, they greet visitors, and Michelle wears a casual but feminine dress by designer Tracy Feith.

Above: Michelle looks on as her husband addresses a joint session of Congress at the Capitol in 2009. Her deep eggplant ensemble, by designer Narciso Rodriguez, shows off those well-toned arms everyone is talking about. **This page, top:** Michelle, center, poses with, from left, Jill Biden, Michelle Fenty, wife of Washington Mayor Adrian Fenty, and Mayor Fenty, outside of Georgia Brown's Restaurant following their lunch, in January 2009, in Washington, D.C. Michelle shows her unabashed love of color in this tone-on-tone layering of two shades of turquoise. **This page, below:** Michelle shakes hands with well-wishers as she departs the restaurant. **Opposite, left:** In this February 2009 photo, Michelle happily models a handmade shawl—in a vivid lavender hue—that she received from Director of Public Affairs for the Bureau of Indian Affairs, Nedra Darling, during an event at the Interior Department in Washington. **Opposite, top right:** Michelle, alongside actor Richard Thomas (left) and actor Jeffrey Wright, during a celebration of the 200th anniversary of the birth of President Lincoln at the grand reopening of Ford's Theatre in Washington in February 2009. Michelle, wearing a full-skirted dress in a unique diagonal plaid, wows. **Opposite, bottom right:** Her earrings added a dazzling sparkle that matched her smile.

Right: Michelle is known for her youthful, modern, easygoing style, and this is a perfect example. She wore this sleeveless dress, a black and cobalt blue sheath, while meeting with White House executive chef Cristeta Comerford, center, and pasty chef Bill Yosses, far right, to discuss the menu for the upcoming Governors' Dinner. **Top:** Michelle, with White House social secretary Desirée Rogers, moments before she speaks at an event to highlight Women's History Month. Michelle's take on basic black is always chic, and this is no exception. The dark hue benefits from layers and textures, and also special touches like a brooch on one shoulder and a wide belt. **Bottom:** Michelle was dressed down but still chic as she left the White House with her husband for a weekend at Camp David.

THE LITTLE BLACK DRESS

The style has been called the LBD by fashion insiders, and from the time it was introduced by Coco Chanel in 1926 it has epitomized chic simplicity. Despite Michelle Obama's love of color and interest in experimentation, she also understands the ease, versatility, and sophistication that a little black dress brings to any occasion. It is the piece no woman should be without, because the power and reliability of basic black will always be in vogue. But what's remarkable about Michelle is her ability to choose styles and shapes wisely so that they become hers and hers alone. Even for the most important photograph of her tenure thus far, her official White House portrait, Michelle chose a classic LBD. Designed by Michael Kors and accessorized with a double strand of pearls, the dress is fitted through the body, slightly flared into an A-line skirt, and cut with armholes that have a slight racer-back line. It is a profound message to the world that she is a strong, secure, modern woman, and it works. This image symbolizes the power of the dress, and more important, the power of the woman in it.

Opposite, bottom left: Here's another take on Michelle's love of the little black dress. This one, a brocade sheath with a bolero jacket topper, is especially elongating. **Opposite, right:** For her official White House photo, Michelle smartly opted for none other than a little black dress. The design, above all others, is always chic, timeless, and flattering. This one, by great American designer Michael Kors, has slight racer-back armholes that emphasize Michelle's well-toned arms. The accessory of choice? A double strand of pearls that offer a radiant glow and a pop of brightness. Perfection. **Above left:** Sleeveless, fitted through the torso, and finished with a ruffled skirt, this little black dress by Tunisian-born French couturier Azzedine Alaia offers high-end glamour. Michelle wore the dress while in Strasbourg, France, for a NATO dinner with heads of state. Critics noted that the choice broke with the tradition of American First Ladies wearing only American designers. **Above right:** The little black dress takes many forms and offers the wearer great flexibility. This sleek, fitted silhouette accentuates Michelle's long, lean frame. The slight boat neck allows a bit of skin to shine through and frame the face. **This page, bottom left:** At the Election Night victory rally at Grant Park in Chicago, Michelle chose what is considered a new version of the little black dress. This one, by designer Narciso Rodriguez, is empire-waisted with a shock of red on the torso. Although some pundits suggested it looked splattered with paint, or, worse yet, blood, the dress was a very fashion-forward choice.

Opposite, left: Michelle, wearing black leggings and a long black sweater (belted, naturally), arrives to plant in the White House kitchen garden. **Opposite, top right:** Michelle was ready for work and dressed for the part. With the help of students from Washington's Bancroft Eementary School, the First Lady happily wielded a rake. **Opposite, bottom right:** Michelle's love of long coats is deep and abiding. The look is a good one, as it's both slimming and camouflaging at the same time. Here, Michelle and Barack leave the White House before departing on their first trip overseas. **This page, top left:** Michelle cheers children on as they play a spelling game at the Old Dominion University Child Study Center in Norfolk, Virginia. Wearing one of her favorite looks—a cardigan sweater over a sheath—she opts for not-so-basic black. **This page, bottom left:** Michelle has mastered the art of layering—top plus cardigan plus jacket—and makes it look effortless. Here, speaking at Arlington National Cemetery's Women in Military Service event, in Arlington, Virginia, she's stylish perfection. **Above:** The Obamas, attending a performance by the Alvin Ailey American Dance Theater at the Kennedy Center. Michelle has said that she now considers Washington, D.C., her home, and to that end she hopes to familiarize herself with all that the city has to offer.

This page, top left: Michelle arrives at the White House East Room to watch her husband sign an executive order to create the White House Council on Women and Girls. Here, she is resplendent in vibrant purple, and shows how cohesive a monochromatic look can be. **This page, top right:** First Lady Michelle arrives at the White House for a performance by schoolchildren. Hers is effortless style, and here she makes a match out of unlikely colors: a pale green sweater and a brown tweed pencil skirt. On her, it works. **This page, bottom left:** First Lady Michelle reads to a group of children of military personnel at the Prager Child Development Center during a trip to Fort Bragg in Fayetteville, North Carolina, in March 2009. **This page, bottom right:** Not only does Michelle embrace color and pattern, she wears it in a bold way. This floral shirtdress won raves from the fashion press. **Opposite, top left:** Michelle is welcomed to Orlando, Florida, by Adult Literacy League volunteers. The sleeveless sheath, a favorite style, is usually worn in a bold color, but here, in white, it looks crisp. **Opposite, top right:** Michelle surprised pupils at the Elizabeth Garrett Anderson School in London with a visit during her April 2009 European tour. For the occasion, she wore an unusual asymmetrical argyle cardigan by designer Junya Watanabe, and a full teal skirt. **Opposite, bottom:** Michelle, with former president Bill Clinton, watching as Barack speaks before the signing of the Edward M. Kennedy Serve America Act in April 2009. Michelle's ability to mix colors—here, black, green, and purple—is a trademark of her fashion flair.

This page, top left: There are many causes to which Michelle is committed, and helping people who have limited or no access to health-care is high on her priority list. Here, she visits Mary's Center, a Washington, D.C., nonprofit that serves those in need. Everything about Michelle's look is right: casual attire and little makeup. That is, except for a pair of green jeweled bow pins at the neckline—a lovely frame for her face. **This page, top right:** A candid shot of Michelle, casually dressed for her speech to high school students at a Washington, D.C., community health center. For a bit of color, she accessorized her cream sweater with a pair of "bow" pins made from faceted green stones. **This page, below left:** Michelle waves to onlookers as she concludes a visit to the Homeland Security Department in Washington. Her vibrant green jacket, belted and pinned with a brooch, is layered over a striped T. It's a mix of casual and pulled together, and a very modern approach. **This page, below right:** While touring an energy-efficient home construction project on the Washington Mall, as part of the YouthBuild's thirtieth anniversary celebration, a dressed-down Michelle looks perfectly at ease. **Opposite, left:** First Lady Michelle plants a tree with volunteers at a national service project at Kenilworth Aquatic Gardens in Washington, D.C. She may have donned gloves for the work, but she is as stylish as ever in a sleeveless shell with green and black ruching detail. **Opposite, top right:** Michelle takes a break from wielding her shovel. An admitted hands-on fanatic, she has shown that same sort of gumption with the projects she has tackled as First Lady. **Opposite, middle right:** Michelle joins Vicki Escarra, president and CEO of Feeding America, for a rally encouraging congressional spouses to assemble bags of food to feed a thousand students who participate in the Food for Kids program in Washington, D.C. The First Lady is suitably dressed down, from her head to her sneaker-adorned feet. **Opposite, bottom right:** Even her sneakers surprise with color. Michelle, dressed for a Feeding America rally, mixes sporty and stylish with gray-and-pink sneakers.

BELTS

In Michelle Obama's fashion notebook, the belt features prominently. Having personal style is a result of many things, but it starts with the understanding of what looks good on you. Michelle has a long frame and a slender waist and she uses belts smartly: they neither pull attention away from the overall look nor are they an insignificant afterthought. What's more, her penchant for belting almost everything— from dresses and cardigans to shirts and coats—has been a mainstay of her wardrobe since she first appeared on the national stage. She has even been known to wear dresses and coats with a banded, beltlike detail incorporated into the design.

This page, top right: President Barack and First Lady Michelle greet the crowd gathered prior to his speech in front of Prague Castle during the couple's European tour in the spring of 2009. A classic white blouse looks bold with its oversized bow, and once again Michelle tops the look with a cardigan and the Sonia Rykiel– designed belt that seems to be a mainstay. **This page, bottom right:** Coming off the plane at the onset of the First Couple's European tour in the spring of 2009, Michelle makes a striking style statement. A canary yellow dress is topped with a long black cardigan (once again, two trends she loves), and finished with what seemed to be a treasured black belt. This one, by French designer Sonia Rykiel, is the perfect width: wide enough to be seen, it also looks proportionate on Michelle's long frame. **Opposite, left:** Michelle's love of belts will likely continue— she's photographed wearing them more often

than not. Here is an unusual example: a wide, clear, plastic belt with a prominent buckle. This belt has made a few appearances, most notably when Michelle appeared on the cover of *O* magazine with friend, supporter, and superstar Oprah Winfrey. **Opposite, top right:** On a casual outing with her family, Michelle maintains her signature style. A basic black top and slim cigarette pants look more finished with a faux snakeskin belt cinching the waist. Easy, effortless, chic. **Opposite, bottom right:** We don't often see Michelle in pants at official events, but when the look is employed it is not without forethought and is always in keeping with her style ideals. Here, a pair of taupe wide-leg pants and a dark top are beautifully accented with a midwidth faux skin belt. It is a prime example of how casual wear, with the right accessories, can look perfectly polished.

This page, left and right: This ensemble, by Thai-born American designer Thakoon Panichgul, was considered edgy by the fashion elite. A study in opposites (the dress is black on fuchsia, the coat is fuchsia on black), the look seems an ideal choice for the Obamas' European tour. **Opposite, top left:** Michelle waves to well-wishers as she leaves Palais Rohan in Strasbourg, France. Her Thakoon-designed dress displays a subtle pattern, but the vibrant hue is hard to miss. **Opposite, bottom left:** On her first tour of Europe as First Lady, Michelle's every fashion move was followed. This chic suit—a black, fitted jacket with wide-leg pants—was designed by Tunisian-born Azzedine Alaia. It's a clear example of how basic black can be anything but basic. **Opposite, right:** Michelle rarely wears pants to official events, but this time she made an exception. Pictured here with France's First Lady, Carla Bruni-Sarkozy, the two women set the bar for how modern First Ladies should look.

Opposite: President Barack Obama and Michelle are escorted by David Walker, the Head of the Household, upon their arrival at Buckingham Palace in London. Michelle is a vision in chic simplicity. **This page, left:** Much was made of the ensemble Michelle wore on her first visit with Britain's Queen Elizabeth. Some thought it too casual; others thought the black-and-white color scheme too stark against the pastel background of Buckingham Palace. **Below:** Michelle and Barack, leaving the British prime minister's residence after a working dinner. There's nothing more classic than black and white, and the skirt's pockets lend a breezy sensibility to the otherwise dressy ensemble.

Opposite: Michelle and Barack appear in Prague, Czech Republic, while on their first trip to Europe. This is a classic look on the First Lady, both casual and chic: a slim black skirt and white blouse should be a part of every woman's wardrobe. After topping it off with a black cardigan, the whole thing gets belted at the waist. **This page, top left:** Michelle, pictured here on a visit to Maggie's Cancer Caring Centre in west London, sticks to styles she knows work well. This jeweled cardigan would work for day or night. **Above:** Walking with Sarah Brown, wife of British prime minister Gordon Brown, Michelle greets onlookers. Her ensemble, from American retailer J.Crew, delighted legions of real women who appreciated her departure from high-end designer wares. **This page, bottom:** It goes to show that a white shirt can be more than a traditional staple. This one, accented with a huge bow at the neck, elevates the top into something altogether unique.

STATEMENT JEWELRY

A pearl necklace is not the only adornment in the Michelle Obama arsenal. Statement pieces—big and bold—are a trend of the moment, and she wears them beautifully. Michelle has ignited an interest in brooches—faux jewel–encrusted vintage-inspired ones—something of a recent addition to fashion runways. The approach, an effortless way to personalize everything from dresses to coats, works best on mature women who have the stature and confidence to wear a big piece of jewelry without its detracting attention from the person wearing it. It's also another great example of fashion forward dressing, as it blurs the line between daywear and night attire. Old thinking: bold at night. New thinking: bold any time.

Opposite, bottom left: Attending a political event with her husband, Michelle elevates a classic red sheath. The V-neckline, flattering for its face-framing appeal, is adorned with three jeweled "bow" pins. The vintage-inspired look is very much a trend. The growing interest in such styling, first seen on designers' runways, tempted many retailers to stock similar pieces, making them available at every price point. Even if your grandmother never left you a single brooch, you can look as if she did. **Opposite, top right:** In an early snapshot of Michelle, long before she emerged as a style icon, she is seen wearing a black and gray checked suit jacket. Already mindful of the effect that one, well-chosen piece of jewelry can have on a look, she accessorizes with a prominent brooch. **Opposite, bottom center:** On the second day of the Democratic National Convention, held in Denver, Colorado, Michelle adorned the pleated front of a taupe dress with three strands of large, bold pearls of mixed color. **Opposite, bottom right:** Addressing the crowd of thousands at the Democratic National Convention in August 2008, Michelle chose a three-quarter-length-sleeved dress that was a standout for its teal color. But the ever-stylish Michelle took the look one step forward by adding a large turquoise stone–encrusted brooch, front and center, at the bottom of the V-neckline. **This page:** Michelle, in black tie attire, attending a formal dinner at the White House for the nation's governors in February 2009. Her strapless dress, a beaded graphite-colored form-fitting gown designed by Peter Sorenon, provided the perfect backdrop for the outstanding multistrand necklace by jewelry designer Tom Binns.

This page, right: Michelle leaves St. John's Episcopal Church with her husband, following Easter Sunday services in 2009. For the occasion, Michelle chose to greet the spring day with a pale, floral dress. She also wears her signature pearls. **This page, bottom right:** The Obama family, heading to the South Lawn of the White House for the annual Easter Egg Roll, April 2009. **This page, bottom left:** A candid moment as Michelle crosses the South Lawn upon returning from a trip to Chicago, her hometown. To ward off the February chill, this double-breasted coat with wide sleeves keeps her warm and chic. **Opposite, top left and right:** Michelle pauses during a ceremonial swearing in for Office of Personnel Management Director John Berry. In her ode to classics-with-a-twist, Michelle wears a cardigan in an unusual color combination, belted with something wide and bold. **Opposite, bottom:** Is it possible Michelle puts the chic in 3-D? Hosting a Super Bowl party in the family theater of the White House, the First Couple dons the paper glasses, while family, friends, staff members, and bipartisan members of Congress join in the fun.

Opposite, top: First Lady Michelle Obama hosts Jordan's Queen Rania in the Yellow Oval Room in the White House Residence in April 2009. Even wearing a dress she's donned before, Michelle gives the über-stylish young Queen a run for her fashion money. **Opposite, bottom left:** First Lady Michelle Obama attends the unveiling ceremony for the bust of Sojourner Truth in the U.S. Capitol Visitors Center later the same day. Michelle elevates a dark shirt dress by choosing one with an element of surprise, here, a swath of bright turquoise. **Opposite, bottom right:** Michelle and Jill Biden arrive at the White House Rose Garden in Washington, D.C., for a ceremony honoring the National Teacher of the Year in April 2009. Of the many unique aspects of Michelle's style, certainly her ability to look both casual and polished, like she does here, is one of her greatest strengths. **This page, left:** Michelle leads the charge as the family takes their dog, Bo, to meet the White House press corp. **Above:** Bo came to the White House with his own flair for fashion.

LONG COATS

The long coat has long been overlooked… until now. One of the most stylish and unique pieces that Michelle Obama uses is the top coat. Worn day and night, it is the finishing touch she employs to unify her looks. Today, there are more lightweight fashionable coats, often termed "car coats," than ever before. The lightweight coat is an ideal layering piece that works almost four seasons a year and is great for traveling because it has less bulk than regular coats. Thus, it is easier to pack and carry. For Michelle, the employment of a coat is with thoughtful consideration: a coat adds an additional layer of interest (in color, texture, design, etc.), it is profoundly useful (warmth) and versatile (coverage), and, above all else, it provides the continuity to finish a look.

Opposite, left: This silk sheath with long top-coat, by Thai-born American designer Thakoon, was worn on the first couple's European tour in April 2009. Both the fabric and the print gave the ensemble a more polished, dressier look, and the fashion press gave it high marks. **Opposite, right:** On the day before Barack Obama's inauguration, a celebration was held on the steps of the Lincoln Memorial. For the event, Michelle looked very much the modern woman in the classic color combination, camel and black. The long coat, warm and chic, is timeless. **This page, top:** Walking to Marine One with Barack for the couple's first overseas tour, Michelle wore a long, cream coat with black bands accenting the border as well as the pockets. A look that was very on-trend at that moment—the classic black-and-white color scheme was featured in nearly every magazine in the spring of 2009—it offered clean lines and a slimming silhouette. **This page, bottom left:** At a rally during the presidential campaign, Michelle's youthful, and some say edgier, side came out. In a departure from her classic long coats, this one was trench coat–like in styling (tied at the waist) and paired with tall black boots—another classic transformed by Michelle's talent for making it her own. **This page, bottom right:** Michelle on her way to dinner at 10 Downing Street, the British prime minister's residence, while on her first European tour at the end of May in 2009. Wearing a full black skirt, white tank, and a long black silk satin evening coat, Michelle evokes a retro style. For any over-forty woman, an evening coat such as this, in a dark hue, can be worn over anything and everything.

The Obama Lifestyle: Casual Elegance

Over the course of many years of President Obama's early Senate campaigning, terms in the Illinois and then the U.S. Senate, and presidential campaigning, Barack and Michelle Obama have created a lifestyle unique to who they are and what their life has been leading them toward. Theirs is a loving partnership within the bubble of their extraordinary life, but it's stressful. Their commitment to each other is a testament to the fact that they both have a deep understanding of their particular journey. It all looks so glamorous on the outside, but of course maintaining a grounded sensibility in the midst of it all isn't easy. Both have spoken openly of the constant communication and understanding necessary to keep it all going. One secret to their marital success? Date night. Some political pundits were outraged when the Obamas would disappear for regular evenings out during the long months of campaigning (well, disappear as much as they could, given their security detail), but the Obamas were not dissuaded. Michelle has been open about the hardship that her husband's political career has, at times, placed on their marriage, and she stood firm in her belief that they would always make together time a priority. Dinner at local restaurants and the occasional movie have been favored destinations, and although the media glare has been intense, the sense remains that these

This page, top left: Malia, 10, and Sasha, 7, arrive at the U.S. Capitol to see their father swear in as president of the United States. **This page, top right:** Hold still, Dad! Malia takes one last picture of her father before he departs for the evening's inaugural festivities. **This page, bottom right:** Getting to 10 parties in a few hours requires fast footwork, or, in this case, finding a ride. Michelle and Barack, pictured here behind the scenes, get the lift they need from a golf cart standing by. **Opposite:** Inauguration night was a long one! Getting in and out of the various inaugural ball venues wasn't always easy, and the First Couple often found themselves in back halls and service elevators. Here, pictured en route and surrounded by their Secret Service detail, Michelle keeps warm with a little help from her husband's tuxedo jacket.

This page, above: Malia, left, and Sasha, emerge from St. John's Church across from the White House where the first family celebrated Easter 2009, in Washington. **This page, top right:** The family after a 2008 caucus rally in Des Moines, Iowa. When asked how she deals with the crowds, Malia, then 9, said according to her mother: "Those people aren't there to see me. They just think I'm cute. So I just wave and smile, and then I'm out of there." **This page, bottom left:** It has been a long time since such a young, vibrant family has lived in the White House. The Obamas, clearly, are loving, hands-on parents to daughters Sasha and Malia. **This page, bottom right:** Sasha, Michelle, and Malia arrive in Chicago looking travel-chic. **Opposite, top left:** The Obama family, dressed in casual attire, deplanes upon arriving in Honolulu, Hawaii, in August 2008. Pundits were stunned that Michelle and Barack scheduled a vacation just when it was coming down to Election Day, but, true to form, the Obamas put family first. **Opposite, bottom left:** Malia, right, takes a picture as she sits next to her sister, Sasha, before their parents arrive onstage at the Lincoln Memorial inaugural concert in January 2009. **Opposite, right:** On a rare, private evening out, Michelle and Barack enjoy a date night. Michelle has been open about the strain on their marriage during her husband's time in the Senate (he lived in Washington during the week while his family lived in Chicago). Now that they're all under one roof—albeit the roof of the White House—Michelle cherishes it.

two people enjoy each other and relish the opportunity to have a "normal" night out.

Which is not to say they don't create normalcy at home. In fact, Michelle has remarked that the surprise silver lining of living in the White House is that they now, for the first time in many years, live together under one roof. Does the president's job call for travel? Of course, but nothing like the weekly back and forth that was required of Barack, between the Obamas' home outside of Chicago and Washington, D.C., when he was in the U.S. Senate, and certainly not nearly the amount of travel miles logged during the presidential campaign.

Home life has always been a central focus for Michelle, and now she has the opportunity to create her ideal environment in the home-of-all-homes, the White House. First order of business? Making the place feel welcome for everyone who works there, which includes numerous members of the house staff. The First Lady has said she wants to hear the sounds of life and laughter of adults as well as children (hers and those of employees). She is not interested in formality for everyday living, and she herself leads the charge by dressing down on days when she doesn't have an official event. She has been photographed taking her children to school and traveling to and from Camp David dressed like every other busy mom: khakis, T-shirts, and her beloved cardigans. On these days, she favors long, lightweight anoraks and the ease and comfort of flats.

And that sensibility carries over to the way Michelle dresses daughters Malia and Sasha. The girls are real kids leading real lives, and Michelle dresses them accordingly. The girls favor jeans and sneakers, just like the rest of their classmates, and also like some girly stuff, too (such as shiny quilted boots or a bright puffy coat). Even on inauguration day Michelle made sure her girls felt comfortable and looked their age. Forget pint-size designer frocks; the Obama daughters looked adorable in coats and scarves from J.Crew.

It's all part of Michelle's plan to maintain a dose of reality at all costs, whether it comes to clothes, playtime, or regular family life. What to expect at home? Sleepovers for the children's classmates, movie nights for friends (not catered with haute cuisine but with family favorites such as pizza and popcorn), and the joyful celebration of holidays and special events. Michelle insists the bookshelves will be stocked with the Harry Potter volumes and *Seventeen* magazines alongside editions of Edith Wharton and Dostoyevsky, and that the music wafting through the halls is as likely to be the Jonas Brothers as it is Mozart.

Like all families with preteens, life in the Obama household is often fun, frivolous, silly, and sometimes a bit chaotic.

It has been reported widely that Michelle has sought and received counsel from previous First Ladies who raised children in the White House, most notably Hilary Clinton (Chelsea was twelve years old when Bill Clinton became president) and Laura Bush (the Bush twins, Jenna and Barbara, were twenty when their family took up residence on Pennsylvania Avenue). Both Mrs. Clinton and Mrs. Bush offered sincere, candid advice, ranging from how to handle the intense media scrutiny to where to score a late-night bowl of ice cream. Although it is a life of extreme access and privilege, it isn't always easy, the women assured Michelle. She took it all in, and took it to heart.

So far, the Obamas have quickly established their own rhythms and routines in their new environs. Michelle has said that they most often eat dinner as a family in the private residence, and that when Barack is in town he almost always tucks the girls in bed at night. Also, the most grounding constant in the Obamas' family life is Michelle's seventy-one-year-old mother, Marian Robinson, who has moved into the White House as well. Robinson has always been an important and present person in the Obama girls' lives, but never more so than during the final months of intense campaigning and the transition from their Chicago home into the White House. She is said to be a guiding force for the entire family, helping with everything involved in keeping a household running—logistics, organization, meals, homework, lessons, playdates, and more.

Of course, a slew of people run the White House. It was reported that White

House staffers were positively giddy at the prospect of having young children in residence again, and visions of ice-cream parties and South Lawn pony rides became daily fodder. But make no mistake that it is Michelle Obama who will remain in charge, as mom-in-chief. The Obama girls will likely spend their years exploring the extensive labyrinth of tunnels and rooms that *is* the sprawling White House, but they will not run wild. On the contrary. It's been reported that Michelle Obama laid down house rules early on, to the girls as well as to the staff that will help take care of them. The girls will be expected to clean their own rooms, make their beds, clear their dishes from the table, and then some. And, now that there's a First Dog in residence, one imagines their caring for Bo will be added to the list. Staffers were cautioned against spoiling the children—certainly there is fun to be had, but Michelle is committed to raising her girls in the manner that she was raised, and that includes homework, chores, rules, and manners.

What is certain is that the Obama family has embarked on the journey of a lifetime. The confidence and steadiness that they've exhibited will serve them and the country well. Expectations may seem impossibly high, but then they always are. It's part of the American sensibility to do better, try harder, and push forward. Certainly the country is facing challenges, but with the Obama message of hope, determination, and change, everyone is looking to a bright future.

Top: The newest member of the Obama household is a Portuguese water dog named Bo. The dog was a gift from Senator Edward Kennedy, and both Michelle and Barack were open about the fact that they promised their girls a dog once the family relocated to Washington. **Bottom:** Part of the Obama formula for keeping their family grounded and organized is Michelle's mother Marian Robinson. A former Spiegel's secretary, Robinson has been helping to raise the girls since they were born, and (reluctantly at first) decided to relocate to Washington and live in the White House.

PHOTO CREDITS

Page 3: Newscom; **Page 6:** Pete Souza/MAI/Landov; **Page 8:** AP Images/Alex Brandon; **Page 10:** Steve Pope/Landov (left); Newscom (top right); AP Images/Charles Dharapak (bottom right); **Page 13:** Newscom; **Page 14:** Newscom (both); **Page 16:** Dennis Brack/Landov (left); **Page 16-17:** Landov; **Page 18:** CBS/Landov (top); Newscom (bottom left); UPI/Laura Cavanaugh/Landov (bottom right); **Page 21:** Newscom; **Page 22:** Newscom; **Page 24:** Polaris; **Page 25:** Newscom (both); **Page 26:** Reuters/Eduardo Munoz/Landov (top); Robert Pitts/Landov (bottom); **Page 27:** MCT/Katrina Wittkamp/Landov; **Page 29:** Newscom (top left); Newscom (bottom left); Newscom (right); **Page 30-31:** Newscom (top left); Reuters/Rick Wilking/Landov (bottom left); Xinhua/Landov (top right); Newscom (bottom right); **Page 32:** AP Images/Chuck Kennedy; **Page 34-35:** Robert Pitts/Landov (bottom left); Newscom (center left); UPI/Ron Sachs/Landov (center right); Newscom (bottom center); The Washington Times/Mary F. Calvert/Landov (left); **Page 37:** Newscom (all); **Page 38-39:** Reuters/Eric Thayer/Landov (left); Reuters/Jason Reed/Landov (center); Reuters/Jim Young/Landov (left); **Page 41:** Newscom; **Page 42:** Reuter/Rick Wilking/Landov (left); MAI/Landov (right); **Page 44:** AP Images/ Haraz N. Ghanbari; **Page 46:** INS News Agency Ltd./Rex Features (top right); Polaris (bottom left and right); **Page 47:** Polaris (top left); INS News Agency Ltd./Rex Features (top right and bottom); **Page 48-49:** AP Images/Douglas Healey (far left); Jason Reed/Reuters/Landov (left); AP Images/Charlie Neibergall (right); AP Images/Charles Rex Arbogast (top right); AP Images/Brennan Linsley (bottom right); **Page 50:** AP Images/Michael A. Mariant (both); **Page 51:** AP Images/Vandell Cobb (top left); AP Images/M. Spencer Green (top right); AP Images/Lawrence Jackson (bottom); **Page 52:** Newscom (left); AP Images/Matt Sayles (top right); Reuters/Jason Reed/Landov (middle right); AP Images/Matt Rourke (bottom right); **Page 53:** Jason Reed/Reuters/Landov (left); Newscom (right); **Page 54:** Newscom (top left); AP Images/Paul Hiffmeyer (top right); John Gress/Reuters/Landov (bottom); **Page 55:** AP Images/Jim Cole (top); Charles Ommanney/Getty Images (bottom left); AP Images/Jae C. Hong (bottom right); **Page 56-57:** AP Images/Ric Francis (left); AP Images/Steven Senne (top right); AP Images/David Zalubowski (bottom right); **Page 58-59:** Jason Reed/Reuters/Landov (left); AP Images/Alex Brandon (center); AP Images/M. Spencer Green (top right); AP Images/Alex Brandon (bottom right); **Page 60:** AP Images/M. Spencer Green (top); AP Images/Elise Amendola (bottom); **Page 61:** AP Images/Jim Cole (left); AP Images/M. Spencer Green (top right); Newscom (bottom right); **Page 62:** Newscom (left and top right); AP Images/Ron Edmonds (bottom right); **Page 63:** Newscom (top left and bottom); AP Images/Jeff Roberson (top right); **Page 64:** Newscom (top left); AP/Brian Ray/Sipa Press (top center); AP Images/Elaine Thompson (top right); Jason Reed/Reuters/Landov (bottom); **Page 65:** Newscom (left); AP Images/Gary Malerba (right); **Page 66:** AP Images/Ted S. Warren (left); AP Images/Jae C. Hong (top right); AP Images/M. Spencer Green (bottom right); **Page 67:** AP Images/Ann Johansson (left); AP Images/ Charles Dharapak (top right); Jason Reed/Reuters/Landov (bottom right); **Page 68:** Reuters/Toby Melville/Landov (left); Ronald Wittek/dpa/Landov (right); **Page 69:** Carl Court/PA Photos/Landov (left); Jason Reed/Reuters/Landov (right); **Page 70:** Newscom (top left & bottom); AP Images/ Darron Cummings (right); **Page 71:** AP Images/Charles Dharapak (left); AP Images/Jae C. Hong (right); **Page 72-73:** AP Images/Charles Dharapak (left); Xinhua/Landov (center); AP Images/Morry Gash (top right); Jason Reed/Reuters/Landov (center right); Eric Miller/Reuters/Landov (bottom right); **Page 74:** AP Images/Jae C. Hong ; **Page 75:** Chuck Kennedy/Getty Images (top left); AP Images/Alex Brandon (top right); AP Images/Alex Brandon (bottom left); Kyodo via AP Images (bottom right); **Page 76:** AP Images/Evan Agostini (top); Reuters/Andrew Parsons/Landov (bottom left); Newscom (bottom right); **Page 77:** Newscom (all); **Page 78:** AP Images/Paul Sancya (top and bottom); **Page 79:** Newscom (left); Reuters/Ellen Ozier/Landov (top right); AP Images/Rick Bowmer (bottom right); **Page 80-81:** Newscom (left); AP Images/Pablo Martinez Monsivais (top right); AP Images/Jae C. Hong (bottom right); **Page 82-83:** Mark Wilson/UPI/Landov (left); Mary F. Calvert/The Washington Times/Landov (center); Hugh Gentry/Reuters/Landov (top right); Jean-Marc Loos/Maxppp/Landov (bottom right); **Page 84-85:** AP Images/Jae C. Hong (top left); Timothy A. Clary/AFP/Getty Images (bottom left); Stan Honda/AFP/Getty Images (right); **Page 86-87:** Chip Somedevilla/Bloomberg News/Landov (left); AP Images/Charles Dharapak (top right); AP Images/Charlie Neibergall (bottom right); **Page 88-89:** Mike Segar/Reuters/Corbis (left); Fiona Hanson/PA Photos/Landov (top center); AP Images/KEvork Djansezian (middle center); Mandi Wright/MCT/Landov (top center); AP Images/Kevork Djansezian (middle center); Mandi Wright/MCT/Landov (bottom center); AP Images/Jae C. Hong (left); **Page 90:** Charles Ommanney/Getty Images (top); Newscom (bottom); **Page 91:** Brooks Kraft/Corbis (top left); Kevin Dietsch/UPI/Landov (top right); Martin H. Simon/Getty Images (bottom); **Page 92:** Newscom (top left); AP Images/Pablo Martinez Monsivais (top right); Kevin LaMarque/Reuters/Corbis (bottom); **Page 93:** AP Images/Lawrence Jackson (left); AP Images/ Evan Vucci (top right); Jason Reed/Reuters/Corbis (bottom right); **Page 94-95:** Kevin LaMarque/Reuters/Landov (top left); Newscom (bottom left and right); **Page 96:** Jessica Rinaldi/Reuters/Landov (left); Newscom (right); **Page 97:** AP Images/Michel Euler (top left); Newscom (top right and bottom); **Page 98:** AP Images/Ron Edmonds (left and top right); Larry Downing/Reuters/Landov (bottom right); **Page 99:** AP Images/Rob Ostermaier (top left); AP Images/Evan Vucci (top right); AP Images/Alex Brandon (bottom); **Page 100:** Ellen Ozier/Reuters/Landov (bottom left); Newscom (top left); Jonathan Ernst/Reuters/Landov (top right); AP Images/Alex Brandon (bottom right); **Page 101:** Newscom (top left and right); Roger L. Wollenberg/UPI/Landov (bottom); **Page 102:** Newscom (top left and bottom right); Joshua Roberts/Reuters/Landov (top right); AP Images/Susan Walsh (bottom left); **Page 103:** AP Images/Charles Dharapak (left); Newscom (top right); Jonathan Ernst/Reuters/Landov (middle and bottom right); **Page 104:** Xinhua/Landov (top); Jim Young/Reuters/Landov (bottom); **Page 105:** AP Images/Pablo Martinez Monsivais (left); Neal Hamberg/Reuters/Landov (top right); AP Images/Jae C. Hong (bottom right); **Page 106:** Philippe Wojazer/Reuters/Landov (left); Hannelore Foerster/Bloomberg News/Landov (right); **Page 107:** Shawn Thew/epa/Corbis (top left); Eric Gaillard/Reuters/Landov (bottom left and right); **Page 108-109:** AP Images/Pablo Martinez Monsivais (left); John Stillwell/Reuters/Landov (center); Newscom (right); **Page 110-111:** Ralf Hirschberger/dpa/Landov (left); Newscom (top center); Thierry Tronnel/Corbis (bottom); Alpha/Landov (top right); **Page 112:** AP Images/Jim Bourg (bottom left); Yuri Gripas/Reuters/Landov (top); AP Images/Ted S. Warren (bottom center); AP Images/Chris Carlson (bottom right); **Page 113:** Mike Theiler/UPI/Landov; **Page 114:** Newscom (all); **Page 115:** AP Images/Evan Vucci (top left); Reuters/Kevin LaMarquee/Landov (top right); Pete Souza/MAI/Landov (bottom); **Page 116-117:** All Newscom except AP Images/The White House, Pete Souza (top right); **Page 118:** Eric Gaillard/Reuters/Landov (left); Scott Strazzante/MCT/Landov (right); **Page 119:** Newscom (top); Rick Wilking/Reuters/Landov (bottom left); AP Images/Pablo Martinez Monsivais (bottom right); **Page 120:** AP Images/Jae C. Hong; **Page 122-123:** AP Images/J. Scott Applewhite (top left); Official White House Photo by Pete Souza (center and bottom, right); **Page 124:** AP Images/J. Scott Applewhite (top left); AP Images/M. Spencer Green (top right); Reuters/Jason Reed/Landov (bottom left); AP Images/Lawrence Jackson (bottom right); **Page 125:** AP Images/Alex Brandon (top left); Newscom (top right); AP Images/Charles Dharapak (bottom); **Page 127:** Jim Young/Reuters/Landov (top); Kevin LaMarque/Reuters/Landov (bottom); **Page 128:** Newscom